MW00512580

FATTY LIVER DIET

MEGA BUNDLE – 5 Manuscripts in 1 – 200+ Recipes designed for a delicious and tasty Fatty liver diet

TABLE OF CONTENTS

ROAST RECIPES 12

ROASTED ZUCCHINI...12

ROASTED SQUASH...13

SOUP RECIPES 14

ZUCCHINI SOUP...14

NOODLE SOUP...15

ROASTED RED PEPPER SOUP 17

POTATO SOUP 19

SIDE DISHES 21

TILAPIA WITH PECAN ROSEMARY 21

CHICKEN THIGHS WITH BRUSSELS SPROUTS AND POTATOES 23

CHICKEN STIR FRY..25

MEATBALLS 26

CHICKEN SALAD SLIDERS..27

CAULIFLOWER RICE 28

CHICKEN THIGHS WITH BUTTERNUT SQUASH 30

TACO LASAGNA 32

GREEN PESTO PASTA...34

OLIVE OIL & HERBS SALMON 35

LEMON CHICKEN THIGHS..36

GARLIC ZUCCHINI 37

CHEESE MACARONI...38

POTATO CASSEROLE..39

CHEESE STUFFED SHELLS..40

CHICKEN ALFREDO 41

PENNE WITH ASPARAGUS..42

TOMATO WRAP...43

THYME COD 44

VEGGIE STIR-FRY 45

RADISHES & ASPARAGUS WITH MINT...46

CRANBERRY SALAD 47

WALDORF SALAD 48

CRANBERRY SALAD 49

GRILLED VEGETABLE SALAD 50

RUSSIAN CABBAGE SALAD 51

ROQUEFORT SALAD 52

BLACK BEAN SALAD 53

CRANBERRY SALAD 54

ARTICHOKE AND WHITE BEAN SALAD..55

STEW RECIPES 56

BEEF STEW 56

IRISH STEW 58

CASSEROLE RECIPES 59

CORN CASSEROLE..59

ARTICHOKE CASSEROLE..61

PIZZA RECIPES 62

CASSEROLE PIZZA 62

BUTTERNUT SQUASH PIZZA 63

SECOND COOKBOOK 64

BREAKFAST 65

BLUEBERRY PANCAKES...65

PEACH PANCAKES 66

BANANA PANCAKES 67

PLUMS PANCAKES 68

PANCAKES 69

MUSHROOM OMELETTE 70

OLIVE OMELETTE..71

ZUCCHINI OMELETTE 72

BASIL OMELETTE 73

MUSHROOM OMELETTE 74

CHEESE OMELETTE 75

STRAWBERRIES OATMEAL 76

BANANA OATMEAL 77

CHERRY-ALMOND OATMEAL 78

SPINACH SCRAMBLE...79

BREAKFAST MIX..80

SAUSAGE BREAKFAST SANDWICH..81

BREAKFAST GRANOLA..82

PANCAKES...83

BLUEBERRY PANCAKES...83

PEACH PANCAKES 84

BANANA PANCAKES 85

PLUMS PANCAKES 86

PANCAKES 87

COOKIES 88

BREAKFAST COOKIES..88

SMOOTHIES 89

CLEMENTINE SMOOTHIE..89

AVOCADO SMOOTHIE 90

PEAR SMOOTHIE 91

BREAKFAST SMOOTHIE 92

BANANA SMOOTHIE..93

GREEN SMOOTHIE..94

KALE SMOOTHIE 95

GREEN JUICE SMOOTHIE 96

SPICY SMOOTHIE 97

COCONUT SMOOTHIE 98

MUFFINS 99

SIMPLE MUFFINS 99

GINGERBREAD MUFFINS 101

KIWI MUFFINS 103

BLUEBERRY MUFFINS 104

PLUM MUFFINS 105

CHOCOLATE MUFFINS 106

PRUNES MUFFINS 107

THIRD COOKBOOK 108

BREAKFAST RECIPES 109

CHOCOLATE COCONUT OATS 109

QUINOA MUESLY WITH COCONUT MILK 110

SWEET POTATO 111

BANANA SPLIT 113

CHAI-SPICED PEAR OATMEAL 114

CHOCOLATE BREAD 116

COCONUT CRACKERS 118

ALMOND BUTTER 120

RAISIN BREAKFAST MIX 122

CRANBERRY BREAKFAST MIX 123

BREAKFAST MIX 124

ACAI PANCAKES 125

AKEE PANCAKES 126

APPLE PANCAKES 127

5

AVOCADO PANCAKES..128

SIMPLE PANCAKES 129

GINGERBREAD MUFFINS..130

BLACKBERRY MUFFINS..131

CHERRY MUFFINS...132

COCONUT MUFFINS..133

CHOCOLATE MUFFINS..134

RAISIN MUFFINS...135

SIMPLE OMELETTE 136

ASPARAGUS OMELETTE 137

BLACK BEANS OMELETTE 138

LENTIL OMELETTE 139

ENDIVE OMELETTE 140

TART RECIPES...141

PEAR TART..141

CARDAMOM TART 143

PIE RECIPES 145

PEACH PECAN PIE...145

BUTTERFINGER PIE...146

STRAWBERRY PIE 147

SMOOTHIE RECIPES 148

APPLE-GINGER SMOOTHIE...148

POMEGRANATE SMOOTHIE 149

MANGO MORNING SMOOTHIE...150

CARAMEL SMOOTHIE...151

BASIL SMOOTHIE 152

PROTEIN SMOOTHIE 153

LOW HISTAMINE SMOOTHIE..154

ICE-CREAM RECIPES 155

PISTACHIOS ICE-CREAM 155

VANILLA ICE-CREAM 157

FOURTH COOKBOOK 158

SIDE DISHES 159

QUINOA FALAFEL 159

VEGAN RAMEN..161

ROASTED CAULIFLOWER 163

GARLIC TOFU 164

BUDDHA BOWL 166

VEGAN RICE BACON 167

FALAFEL BITES 168

ZUCCHINI FRIES 169

ZUCCHINI DAL 170

CHICKPEA PATTIES 171

ONION SOUP 172

ZUCCHINI SOUP..173

SAUERKRAUT SOUP...174

GREEK RICE SOUP 176

SALMON PIZZA 178

GREEN OLIVE PIZZA 179

CAULIFLOWER PIZZA 180

ARTICHOKE AND SPINACH PIZZA 181

BEANS FRITATTA 182

SPINACH FRITATTA..183

ASIAN GREENS FRITATTA 184

SALAMI FRITATTA..185

BROCCOLI FRITATTA..186

VEGETARIAN CARBONARA 187

KALE & QUINOA BOWL 188

AVOCADO TOAST 189

FIG & BRIE GRILLED CHEESE 190

ROASTED SQUASH..191

BRUSSELS SPROUT CHIPS 192

PASTA..193

SIMPLE SPAGHETTI..193

CHICKEN PASTA 195

SHRIMP PASTA 196

PASTA WITH OLIVES AND TOMATOES 197

SALAD RECIPES 198

GREEN SALAD WITH THAI DRESSING 198

CRANBERRY KALE SALAD..199

AVOCADO AND SHRIMP SALAD 200

FENNEL SALAD 201

CRANBERRY SALAD 202

GREEN SALAD..203

CUCUMBER SALAD 204

APRICOT SALAD...205

MORNING SALAD 206

FIFTH COOKBOOK..207

SOUP RECIPES 208

ZUCCHINI SOUP...208

CUCUMBER SOUP 210

VEGETARIAN MINESTRONE SOUP 211

CABBAGE STEW...213

CHICKEN RICE SOUP 214

MISO SOUP 216

MUSHROOM SOUP 218

CHICKEN SOUP 219

ASPARAGUS SOUP 221

SEASWEED SOUP 223

SIDE DISHES 224

SESAME PORK TACOS 224

WATERMELON GAZPACHO 226

LIME GRILLED CORN 227

MACADAMIA DIP WITH VEGETABLES 228

GINGERSNAPS 229

TURKEY & VEGGIES STUFFED PEPPERS 231

QUINOA TACO MEAT 233

KALE CHIPS 235

CHICKEN AND BROWN RICE PASTA 236

PHILLY CHEESE STEAK 237

CAULIFLOWER WINGS 239

ROASTED BOK CHOY 241

GREEN PESTO PASTA 242

TACO SALAD 243

KALE SALAD 244

ROASTED LOW HISTAMNE SALAD 245

PUMPKIN SALAD 246

RED CHICORY SALAD 247

FENNEL SALAD 248

GIGNER CILANTRO SALAD 249

WATERCRESS FRITATTA 250

KALE FRITATTA 251

9

MEDITERRANENA BUDDA BOWL 252

VEGAN CURRY 254

CAULIFLOWER WITH ROSEMARY 256

BRUSSELS SPROUTS..257

PIZZA 258

SIMPLE PIZZA RECIPE 258

ZUCCHINI PIZZA..259

CAULIFLOWER RECIPE 260

BROCCOLI RECIPE..261

TOMATOES & HAM PIZZA 262

Introduction

Fatty Liver recipes for personal enjoyment but also for family enjoyment. You will love them for sure for how easy it is to prepare them.

ROASTED ZUCCHINI

Serves: **3-4**
Prep Time: **10**   Minutes

Cook Time: **20**   Minutes

Total Time: **30**   Minutes

INGREDIENTS

- 2 lb. zucchini
- 2 tablespoons olive oil
- 1 tsp curry powder
- 1 tsp salt

DIRECTIONS

1. Preheat the oven to 400 F
2. Cut everything in half lengthwise
3. Toss everything with olive oil and place onto a prepared baking sheet
4. Roast for 18-20 minutes at 400 F or until golden brown
5. When ready remove from the oven and serve

Serves: **3-4**

Prep Time: **10**   Minutes

Cook Time: **20**   Minutes

Total Time: **30**   Minutes

INGREDIENTS

- 2 delicata squashes
- 2 tablespoons olive oil
- 1 tsp curry powder
- 1 tsp salt

DIRECTIONS

1. Preheat the oven to 400 F
2. Cut everything in half lengthwise
3. Toss everything with olive oil and place onto a prepared baking sheet
4. Roast for 18-20 minutes at 400 F or until golden brown
5. When ready remove from the oven and serve

ZUCCHINI SOUP

Serves: **4**

Prep Time: **10**   Minutes

Cook Time: **20**   Minutes

Total Time: **30**   Minutes

INGREDIENTS

- 1 tablespoon olive oil
- 1 lb. zucchini
- ¼ red onion
- ½ cup all-purpose flour
- ¼ tsp salt
- ¼ tsp pepper
- 1 can vegetable broth
- 1 cup heavy cream

DIRECTIONS

1. In a saucepan heat olive oil and sauté zucchini until tender
2. Add remaining ingredients to the saucepan and bring to a boil
3. When all the vegetables are tender transfer to a blender and blend until smooth
4. Pour soup into bowls, garnish with parsley and serve

Serves: **4**

Prep Time: **10** Minutes

Cook Time: **20** Minutes

Total Time: **30** Minutes

INGREDIENTS

- 2-3 cups water
- 1 can chicken broth
- 1 tablespoon olive oil
- ¼ red onion
- ¼ cup celery
- ¼ tsp salt
- ¼ tsp black pepper
- 5-6 oz. fusilli pasta
- 2 cups chicken breast
- 2 tablespoons parsley

DIRECTIONS

1. In a pot boil water with broth
2. In a saucepan heat oil, add carrot, pepper, celery, onion, salt and sauté until tender
3. Add broth mixture to the mixture and pasta

4. Cook until al dente and stir in chicken breast, cook until chicken breast is tender

5. When ready remove from heat, stir in parsley and serve

ROASTED RED PEPPER SOUP

Serves: **6**

Prep Time: **30** Minutes

Cook Time: **30** Minutes

Total Time: **60** Minutes

INGREDIENTS

- 4 cups vegetable broth
- 1 can green chiles
- 2 tsp cumin
- 2 tbs fresh cilantro
- 1 tbs lemon juice
- 4 ounces cream cheese
- 2 tbs olive oil
- 2 onions
- 1 jar roasted red peppers
- 2 tsp salt
- 1 tsp coriander
- 4 cups sweet potatoes

DIRECTIONS

1. Heat the oil in a pan.
2. Cook the onions until soft, then add the peppers, green chiles, coriander, cumin, and salt and cook for 3 minutes.

3. Stir in the roasted peppers juice, peeled and cubed potatoes, and the vegetable broth.
4. Bring to a boil, then reduce the heat and cook for 15 minutes.
5. Stir in the lemon juice and cilantro.
6. Blend half of the soup with the cream cheese, then add back into the soup, serve immediately.

POTATO SOUP

Serves: **4-6**

Prep Time: **10** Minutes

Cook Time: **50** Minutes

Total Time: **60** Minutes

INGREDIENTS

- 1 onion
- 2-3 carrots
- 2 tablespoons flour
- 5-6 large potatoes
- 2 cups milk
- 2 cups bouillon
- 1 cup water
- 2 cups milk
- 1 tsp salt
- 1 tsp pepper

DIRECTIONS

1. In a saucepan melt butter and sauce carrots, garlic and onion for 4-5 minutes

2. Add flour, milk, potatoes, bouillon and cook for another 15-20 minutes

3. Add pepper and remaining ingredients and cook on low heat for 20-30 minutes

4. When ready remove from heat and serve

SIDE DISHES

TILAPIA WITH PECAN ROSEMARY

Serves: **4**

Prep Time: **20**   Minutes

Cook Time: **20**   Minutes

Total Time: **40**   Minutes

INGREDIENTS

- Cayenne pepper
- 1/3 cup breadcrumbs
- 2 tsp rosemary
- 1 ½ tsp olive oil
- 1 egg white
- 1/3 cup pecans
- 4 tilapia fillets
- ½ tsp brown sugar
- 1/8 tsp salt

DIRECTIONS

1. Preheat the oven to 350F.
2. Stir together the sugar, cayenne pepper, rosemary, pecans, breadcrumbs, and salt.
3. Add the olive oil and toss.
4. Bake for 10 minutes.

5. Whisk the egg white in a bowl and dip the fish into it then into the pecan mixture.

6. Bake for 10 minutes.

7. Serve immediately.

CHICKEN THIGHS WITH BRUSSELS SPROUTS AND POTATOES

Serves: **4**

Prep Time: **15** Minutes

Cook Time: **30** Minutes

Total Time: **45** Minutes

INGREDIENTS

- 2 tsp salt
- 1 tsp thyme
- 1 lb chicken thighs
- 1 lb potatoes
- 3 tbs olive oil
- 1 lemon
- 1 orange
- 1 tsp black pepper
- 2 cloves garlic
- 4 shallots
- 1 ½ tbs paprika
- 2 lb Brussels sprouts

DIRECTIONS

1. Preheat the oven to 450F.
2. Toss the Brussels sprouts, potatoes, shallots, lemon and orange slices with 1 tbs oil, 1 tsp salt, and ½ tsp pepper.

3. Pour into a baking dish.

4. Mix the garlic, remaining salt and pepper, thyme, lemon and orange zest, paprika, and 2 tsp oil in a bowl.

5. Toss the chicken into the mixture.

6. Place the chicken over the Brussels sprouts.

7. Roast for 25 minutes, then serve.

CHICKEN STIR FRY

Serves: **2**

Prep Time: **10**   Minutes

Cook Time: **10**   Minutes

Total Time: **20**   Minutes

INGREDIENTS

- 2 bell peppers
- 2 chicken breasts
- 1 tsp cumin
- 1 tsp cayenne pepper
- 1 tsp olive oil
- ½ tsp paprika
- 2 cups broccoli florets

DIRECTIONS

1. Heat the oil in a pan.
2. Add the diced chicken and cook until browned.
3. Add the broccoli and peppers and cook for 5-10 minutes.
4. Add the spices and a little water.
5. Cook for another few minutes.

Serves: *8*

Prep Time: *15*   Minutes

Cook Time: *20*   Minutes

Total Time: *35*   Minutes

INGREDIENTS

- 3 tbs ketchup
- ½ cup breadcrumbs
- 2 garlic cloves
- 2 tsp salt
- 1 lb ground beef
- ½ cup onion
- 1 tsp pepper
- 1 ½ tbs parsley
- 1 egg
- ½ cup cheese

DIRECTIONS

1. Preheat the oven to 400F.
2. Mix all of the ingredients in a bowl.
3. Form balls and place them on a greased cookie sheet.
4. Cook for 20 minutes, allow to cool, then serve.

CHICKEN SALAD SLIDERS

Serves: **4**

Prep Time: **10**   Minutes

Cook Time: **0**   Minutes

Total Time: **10**   Minutes

INGREDIENTS

- ¼ cup almonds
- 1 cup apples
- ¼ cup dried cranberries
- 1 tsp salt
- 4 buns
- ½ lb shredded rotisserie chicken
- ¾ cup Greek yogurt
- 1 cup grapes

DIRECTIONS

1. Combine all of the ingredients in a bowl, except the buns.
2. Place the mixture onto the buns and secure with a toothpick, serve immediately.

Serves: **4**

Prep Time: **10**   Minutes

Cook Time: **20**   Minutes

Total Time: **30**   Minutes

INGREDIENTS

- 2 tbs soy sauce
- ½ tsp sesame oil
- ½ onion
- 2 cloves garlic
- 1 cup carrots
- 1 tsp black pepper
- 1 cauliflower
- 1 egg
- 2 Tbs oil
- 2 green onions
- 2 tsp salt
- 1 cup peas

DIRECTIONS

1. Mince the cauliflower.
2. Cook the onion and garlic in the oil in a pan.
3. Add the cauliflower and sauté.

4. Add the peas and carrots and stir until combined.

5. Add the sesame oil, soy sauce, beaten egg, and black pepper.

6. Stir until well cooked.

7. Add green onions, season, stir and serve.

CHICKEN THIGHS WITH BUTTERNUT SQUASH

Serves: **6**
Prep Time: **20** Minutes

Cook Time: **30** Minutes

Total Time: **50** Minutes

INGREDIENTS

- ½ lb bacon
- Pepper
- 3 cup Butternut Squash
- 2 tbs oil
- 6 chicken thighs
- Sage
- Salt

DIRECTIONS

1. Preheat the oven to 425F.
2. Fry the bacon until crispy.
3. Sauté the butternut squash in the bacon grease.
4. Season and cook until soft, then remove.
5. Cook the chicken thighs for 10 minutes.
6. Flip the thighs over and add the butternut all around.
7. Place the skillet in the oven.
8. Bake for 15 minutes.

9. Serve topped with the bacon and sage.

TACO LASAGNA

Serves: **9**

Prep Time: **20** Minutes

Cook Time: **30** Minutes

Total Time: **50** Minutes

INGREDIENTS

- 3 cup cheese
- 2/3 cup water
- 1 can tomatoes
- ½ cup green pepper
- 1 lb ground beef
- taco seasoning
- 1 can black beans
- ½ cup chopped onion
- 6 tortillas
- 1 can refried beans

DIRECTIONS

1. Cook the beef, onion, and pepper over medium heat.
2. Add the taco seasoning and water and bring to a boil.
3. Stir in the tomatoes and black beans.
4. Simmer for 10 minutes.

5. Place 2 tortillas into a baking dish and spread half of the mixture over.

6. Sprinkle 1 cup cheese and repeat layers.

7. Top with cheese.

8. Cook until the cheese it melted for about 30 minutes.

9. Serve immediately.

Serves: 2
Prep Time: 5   Minutes

Cook Time: 15   Minutes

Total Time: 20   Minutes

INGREDIENTS

- 4 oz. spaghetti
- 2 cups basil leaves
- 2 garlic cloves
- ¼ cup olive oil
- 2 tablespoons parmesan cheese
- ½ tsp black pepper

DIRECTIONS

1. Bring water to a boil and add pasta
2. In a blend add parmesan cheese, basil leaves, garlic and blend
3. Add olive oil, pepper and blend again
4. Pour pesto onto pasta and serve when ready

OLIVE OIL & HERBS SALMON

Serves: **4**

Prep Time: **15**   Minutes

Cook Time: **40**   Minutes

Total Time: **55**   Minutes

INGREDIENTS

- ½ cup oil
- 1 ½ lb salmon
- ¼ cup dill fronds
- ¼ cup tarragon leaves
- 1 lemon zest
- 1 shallot
- Salt
- Pepper

DIRECTIONS

1. Preheat the oven to 250F.
2. Cook the salmon in the oil in a large pan.
3. Process the dill, lemon zest, shallot and tarragon in a food processor.
4. Blend in 2 tbs of oil and pour the paste over the salmon.
5. Bake for 30 minutes and serve with green salad.

LEMON CHICKEN THIGHS

Serves: *4*
Prep Time: *10*   Minutes

Cook Time: *30*   Minutes

Total Time: *40*   Minutes

INGREDIENTS

- 5 thyme sprigs
- Salt
- Pepper
- 2 lb chicken thighs
- Oil
- 1 lemon

DIRECTIONS

1. Preheat the oven to 400F.
2. Drizzle oil over the chicken and season with salt and pepper.
3. Cook over medium heat for 15 minutes.
4. When crispy, flip over and scatter lemon slices and thyme over.
5. Roast for another 15 minutes.
6. Serve immediately.

GARLIC ZUCCHINI

Serves: **4**

Prep Time: **20** Minutes

Cook Time: **30** Minutes

Total Time: **50** Minutes

INGREDIENTS

- 3 tbs basil
- 1/3 cup oil
- ¼ cup red wine vinegar
- 2 lb zucchini
- Salt
- Pepper
- ¼ cup parsley
- 3 cloves garlic

DIRECTIONS

1. Sprinkle the zucchini with salt, let stand for 30 minutes, then rinse.
2. Mix the basil, parsley, and garlic in a bowl.
3. Fry the zucchini in the oil for about 5 minutes.
4. Transfer the zucchini to a plate and top with the herb mixture and the vinegar.
5. Season with salt and pepper.

CHEESE MACARONI

Serves: *1*
Prep Time: *10* Minutes

Cook Time: *20* Minutes

Total Time: *30* Minutes

INGREDIENTS

- 1 lb. macaroni
- 1 cup cheddar cheese
- 1 cup Monterey Jack cheese
- 1 cup mozzarella cheese
- ¼ tsp salt
- ¼ tsp pepper

DIRECTIONS

1. In a pot bring water to a boil
2. Add pasta and cook until al dente
3. In a bowl combine all cheese together and add it to the pasta
4. When ready transfer to a bowl, add salt, pepper and serve

POTATO CASSEROLE

Serves: 2

Prep Time: **10**   Minutes

Cook Time: **20**   Minutes

Total Time: **30**   Minutes

INGREDIENTS

- 5-6 large potatoes
- ¼ cup sour cream
- ½ cup butter
- 5-6 bacon strips
- 1-2 cups mozzarella cheese
- ¼ cup heavy cream

DIRECTIONS

1. Place the potatoes in a pot with boiling water, cook until tender
2. Place the potatoes in a bowl, add sour cream, butter, cheese and mix well
3. In a baking dish place the bacon strips and cover with potato mixture
4. Add remaining mozzarella cheese on top
5. Bake at 325 F for 15-18 minutes or until the mozzarella is fully melted
6. When ready remove from the oven and serve

CHEESE STUFFED SHELLS

Serves: **2**

Prep Time: **10** Minutes

Cook Time: **30** Minutes

Total Time: **40** Minutes

INGREDIENTS

- 2-3 cups macaroni
- 2 cups cream cheese
- 1 cup spaghetti sauce
- 1 cup onions
- 1 cup mozzarella cheese

DIRECTIONS

1. In a pot boil water and add shells
2. Cook for 12-15 minutes
3. In a baking dish add spaghetti sauce
4. In a bowl combine cream cheese, onion and set aside
5. Add cream cheese to the shells and place them into the baking dish
6. Bake at 325 F for 30 minutes or until golden brown
7. When ready remove from the oven and serve

CHICKEN ALFREDO

Serves: **2**
Prep Time: **10**   Minutes

Cook Time: **20**   Minutes

Total Time: **30**   Minutes

INGREDIENTS

- 2-3 chicken breasts
- 1 lb. rotini
- 1 cup parmesan cheese
- 1 cup olive oil
- 1 tsp salt
- 1 tsp black pepper
- 1 tsp parsley

DIRECTIONS

1. In a pot add the rotini and cook on low heat for 12-15 minutes
2. In a frying pan heat olive oil, add chicken, salt, parsley, and cook until the chicken is brown
3. Drain the rotini and place the rotini in pan with chicken
4. Cook for 2-3 minutes
5. When ready remove from heat and serve with parmesan cheese on top

PENNE WITH ASPARAGUS

Serves: **2**

Prep Time: **10**   Minutes

Cook Time: **20**   Minutes

Total Time: **30**   Minutes

INGREDIENTS

- 6-7 oz. penne pasta
- 2-3 bacon slices
- ¼ cup red onion
- 2 cups asparagus
- 1 cup chicken broth
- 2-3 cups spinach leaves
- ¼ cup parmesan cheese

DIRECTIONS

1. Cook pasta until al dente
2. In a skillet cook bacon until crispy and set aside
3. In a pan add onion, asparagus, broth and cook on low heat for 5-10 minutes
4. Add spinach, cheese, pepper, pasta and cook for another 5-6 minutes
5. When ready sprinkle bacon and serve

TOMATO WRAP

Serves: **4**

Prep Time: **5**   Minutes

Cook Time: **15**   Minutes

Total Time: **20**   Minutes

INGREDIENTS

- 1 cup corn
- 1 cup tomatoes
- 1 cup pickles
- 1 tablespoon olive oil
- 1 tablespoon mayonnaise
- 6-7 turkey slices
- 2-3 whole-wheat tortillas
- 1 cup romaine lettuce

DIRECTIONS

1. In a bowl combine tomatoes, pickles, olive oil, corn and set aside
2. Place the turkey slices over the tortillas and top with tomato mixture and mayonnaise
3. Roll and serve

THYME COD

Serves: 2
Prep Time: 5   Minutes

Cook Time: 15   Minutes

Total Time: 20   Minutes

INGREDIENTS

- 1 tablespoon olive oil
- ½ red onion
- 1 can tomatoes
- 2-3 springs thyme
- 2-3 cod fillets

DIRECTIONS

1. In a frying pan heat olive oil and sauté onion, stir in tomatoes, spring thyme and cook for 5-6 minutes
2. Add cod fillets, cover and cook for 5-6 minutes per side
3. When ready remove from heat and serve

VEGGIE STIR-FRY

Serves: **2**
Prep Time: **10** Minutes

Cook Time: **20** Minutes

Total Time: **30** Minutes

INGREDIENTS

- 1 tablespoon cornstarch
- 1 garlic clove
- ¼ cup olive oil
- ¼ head broccoli
- ¼ cup show peas
- ½ cup carrots
- ¼ cup green beans
- 1 tablespoon soy sauce
- ½ cup onion

DIRECTIONS

1. In a bowl combine garlic, olive oil, cornstarch and mix well
2. Add the rest of the ingredients and toss to coat
3. In a skillet cook vegetables mixture until tender
4. When ready transfer to a plate garnish with ginger and serve

RADISHES & ASPARAGUS WITH MINT

Serves: **4**

Prep Time: **10**   Minutes

Cook Time: **3**   Minutes

Total Time: **40**   Minutes

INGREDIENTS

- 1 ½ tsp vinegar
- ½ tbs butter
- Salt
- Pepper
- 1 lb asparagus
- ¼ cup mint leaves
- 4 ounces radishes
- 1 tbs oil

DIRECTIONS

1. Cut the asparagus into pieces.
2. Cook the asparagus for 3 minutes in the butter.
3. Slice the radishes and toss with the asparagus in a bowl.
4. Mix the oil and the vinegar and pour the mixture over the vegetables.
5. Season with salt and pepper.
6. Slice the mint and toss with the vegetables, serve cold.

CRANBERRY SALAD

Serves: 2

Prep Time: 5   Minutes

Cook Time: 15   Minutes

Total Time: 20   Minutes

INGREDIENTS

- ½ cup celery
- 1 packet Knox Gelatin
- 1 cup cranberry juice
- 1 can berry cranberry sauce
- 1 cup sour cream

DIRECTIONS

1. In a pan add juice, gelatin, cranberry sauce and cook on low heat
2. Add sour cream, celery and continue to cook
3. Pour mixture into a pan
4. Serve when ready

Serves: *2*
Prep Time: *5*   Minutes

Cook Time: *5*   Minutes

Total Time: *10* Minutes

INGREDIENTS

- 1 tablespoon mayonnaise
- 1 tablespoon lemon juice
- 1 apple
- 1 cup red grapes
- ½ cup cranberries
- ½ cup walnuts
- 12 cup celery
- 6 lettuce leaves

DIRECTIONS

1. In a bowl combine all ingredients together and mix well
2. Serve with dressing

CRANBERRY SALAD

Serves: **2**

Prep Time: **5** Minutes

Cook Time: **5** Minutes

Total Time: **10** Minutes

INGREDIENTS

- 1 can unsweetened pineapple
- 1 package cherry gelatin
- 1 tablespoon lemon juice
- ½ cup artificial sweetener
- 1 cup cranberries
- 1 orange
- 1 cup celery
- ½ cup pecans

DIRECTIONS

1. In a bowl combine all ingredients together and mix well
2. Serve with dressing

Serves: 2

Prep Time: 5   Minutes

Cook Time: 5   Minutes

Total Time: *10* Minutes

INGREDIENTS

- ¼ lb. asparagus
- 1 zucchini
- 1 yellow squash
- ¼ red onion
- 1 red bell pepper
- ¼ cup olive oil
- ¼ cup red wine vinegar
- 2 garlic cloves
- Salt

DIRECTIONS

1. Cut into thin strips and grill all vegetables
2. In a bowl mix all ingredients and mix well
3. Serve with salad dressing

Serves: **2**

Prep Time: **5**   Minutes

Cook Time: **5**   Minutes

Total Time: **10** Minutes

INGREDIENTS

- 2 lb. cabbage
- 2 carrots
- 2 beets
- 2 garlic cloves
- ¼ tsp black pepper
- ¼ cup olive oil

DIRECTIONS

1. In a bowl combine all ingredients together and mix well
2. Serve with dressing

ROQUEFORT SALAD

Serves: 2

Prep Time: 5   Minutes

Cook Time: 5   Minutes

Total Time: 10   Minutes

INGREDIENTS

- 1 head leaf lettuce
- 2 pears
- 4 oz. Roquefort cheese
- 1 avocado
- ¼ cup green onions
- ¼ cup pecans
- ¼ cup olive oil
- 1 tsp mustard
- 1 garlic clove
- ¼ tsp salt

DIRECTIONS

1. In a bowl combine all ingredients together and mix well
2. Serve with dressing

BLACK BEAN SALAD

Serves: 2

Prep Time: 5   Minutes

Cook Time: 5   Minutes

Total Time: *10*   Minutes

INGREDIENTS

- 1 can black beans
- 1 can corn
- 4 green onion
- 1 red bell pepper
- 2 tomatoes
- 1 lime
- ¼ cup salad dressing

DIRECTIONS

1. In a bowl combine all ingredients together and mix well
2. Serve with dressing

Serves: 2
Prep Time: 5   Minutes

Cook Time: 5   Minutes

Total Time: 10 Minutes

INGREDIENTS

- 1 can unsweetened pineapple
- 1 package cherry gelatin
- 1 tablespoon lemon juice
- ½ cup artificial sweetener
- 1 cup cranberries
- 1 orange
- 1 cup celery
- ½ cup pecans

DIRECTIONS

1. In a bowl mix all ingredients and mix well
2. Serve with dressing

Serves: **2**

Prep Time: **5** Minutes

Cook Time: **5** Minutes

Total Time: **10** Minutes

INGREDIENTS

- 2 cups white beans
- ¼ can artichoke hearts
- ¼ cup red bell pepper
- ¼ cup black olives
- ½ cup red onion
- ¼ cup parsley
- Mint leaves
- ¼ cup olive oil

DIRECTIONS

1. In a bowl combine all ingredients together and mix well
2. Serve with dressing

STEW RECIPES

BEEF STEW

Serves: **4**

Prep Time: **15**   Minutes

Cook Time: **45**   Minutes

Total Time: **60**   Minutes

INGREDIENTS

- 2 lb. beef
- 1 tsp salt
- 4 tablespoons olive oil
- 2 red onions
- 2 cloves garlic
- 1 cup white wine
- 2 cups beef broth
- 1 cup water
- 3-4 bay leaves
- ¼ tsp thyme
- 1 lb. potatoes

DIRECTIONS

1. Chop all ingredients in big chunks
2. In a large pot heat olive oil and add ingredients one by one

3. Cook for 5-6 or until slightly brown
4. Add remaining ingredients and cook until tender, 35-45 minutes
5. Season while stirring on low heat
6. When ready remove from heat and serve

IRISH STEW

Serves: **4**

Prep Time: **15**   Minutes

Cook Time: **45**   Minutes

Total Time: **60**   Minutes

INGREDIENTS

- 4-5 slices bacon
- 2 lb. beef
- ¼ cup flour
- ½ tsp black pepper
- 4 carrots
- ½ cup beef broth

DIRECTIONS

1. Chop all ingredients in big chunks
2. In a large pot heat olive oil and add ingredients one by one
3. Cook for 5-6 or until slightly brown
4. Add remaining ingredients and cook until tender, 35-45 minutes
5. Season while stirring on low heat
6. When ready remove from heat and serve

CORN CASSEROLE

Serves: **4**

Prep Time: **10**   Minutes

Cook Time: **15**   Minutes

Total Time: **25**   Minutes

INGREDIENTS

- ½ cup cornmeal
- ½ cup butter
- 2 eggs
- 1 cup milk
- ½ cup heavy cream
- 3 cups corn
- ¼ tsp smoked paprika

DIRECTIONS

1. Sauté the veggies and set aside
2. Preheat the oven to 425 F
3. Transfer the sautéed veggies to a baking dish, add remaining ingredients to the baking dish
4. Mix well, add seasoning and place the dish in the oven

5. Bake for 12-15 minutes or until slightly brown
6. When ready remove from the oven and serve

ARTICHOKE CASSEROLE

Serves: **4**

Prep Time: **10**   Minutes

Cook Time: **15**   Minutes

Total Time: **25**   Minutes

INGREDIENTS

- 1 cup cooked rice
- 1 cup milk
- 1 cup parmesan cheese
- 4 oz. cream cheese
- 1 lb. cooked chicken breast
- 1 cup spinach
- 1 can artichoke hearts
- 1 cup mozzarella cheese

DIRECTIONS

1. Sauté the veggies and set aside
2. Preheat the oven to 425 F
3. Transfer the sautéed veggies to a baking dish, add remaining ingredients to the baking dish
4. Mix well, add seasoning and place the dish in the oven
5. Bake for 12-15 minutes or until slightly brown
6. When ready remove from the oven and serve

CASSEROLE PIZZA

Serves: **6-8**

Prep Time: **10**   Minutes

Cook Time: **15**   Minutes

Total Time: **25**   Minutes

INGREDIENTS

- 1 pizza crust
- ½ cup tomato sauce
- ¼ black pepper
- 1 cup zucchini slices
- 1 cup mozzarella cheese
- 1 cup olives

DIRECTIONS

1. Spread tomato sauce on the pizza crust
2. Place all the toppings on the pizza crust
3. Bake the pizza at 425 F for 12-15 minutes
4. When ready remove pizza from the oven and serve

BUTTERNUT SQUASH PIZZA

Serves: **4-6**

Prep Time: **10**   Minutes

Cook Time: **15**   Minutes

Total Time: **25**   Minutes

INGREDIENTS

- 2 cups butternut squash
- ¼ tsp salt
- 1 pizza crust
- 5-6 tablespoons alfredo sauce
- 1 tsp olive oil
- 4-5 cups baby spinach
- 2-3 oz. goat cheese

DIRECTIONS

1. Place the pizza crust on a baking dish and spread the alfredo sauce
2. In a skillet sauté spinach and place it over the pizza crust
3. Add goat cheese, butternut squash, olive oil and salt
4. Bake pizza at 425 F for 8-10 minutes
5. When ready remove from the oven and serve

SECOND COOKBOOK

BLUEBERRY PANCAKES

Serves: **4**

Prep Time: **10**   Minutes

Cook Time: **20**   Minutes

Total Time: **30**   Minutes

INGREDIENTS

- 1 cup whole wheat flour
- ¼ tsp baking soda
- ¼ tsp baking powder
- 1 cup blueberries
- 2 eggs
- 1 cup milk

DIRECTIONS

1. In a bowl combine all ingredients together and mix well
2. In a skillet heat olive oil
3. Pour ¼ of the batter and cook each pancake for 1-2 minutes per side
4. When ready remove from heat and serve

Serves: **4**

Prep Time: **10**   Minutes

Cook Time: **30**   Minutes

Total Time: **40**   Minutes

INGREDIENTS

- 1 cup whole wheat flour
- ¼ tsp baking soda
- ¼ tsp baking powder
- 1 cup mashed peaches
- 2 eggs
- 1 cup milk

DIRECTIONS

1. In a bowl combine all ingredients together and mix well
2. In a skillet heat olive oil
3. Pour ¼ of the batter and cook each pancake for 1-2 minutes per side
4. When ready remove from heat and serve

BANANA PANCAKES

Serves: **4**

Prep Time: **10**   Minutes

Cook Time: **20**   Minutes

Total Time: **30**   Minutes

INGREDIENTS

- 1 cup whole wheat flour
- ¼ tsp baking soda
- ¼ tsp baking powder
- 1 cup mashed banana
- 2 eggs
- 1 cup milk

DIRECTIONS

1. In a bowl combine all ingredients together and mix well
2. In a skillet heat olive oil
3. Pour ¼ of the batter and cook each pancake for 1-2 minutes per side
4. When ready remove from heat and serve

PLUMS PANCAKES

Serves: **4**

Prep Time: **10**   Minutes

Cook Time: **20**   Minutes

Total Time: **30**   Minutes

INGREDIENTS

- 1 cup whole wheat flour
- ¼ tsp baking soda
- ¼ tsp baking powder
- 1 cup mashed plums
- 2 eggs
- 1 cup milk

DIRECTIONS

1. In a bowl combine all ingredients together and mix well
2. In a skillet heat olive oil
3. Pour ¼ of the batter and cook each pancake for 1-2 minutes per side
4. When ready remove from heat and serve

PANCAKES

Serves: **4**

Prep Time: **10** Minutes

Cook Time: **30** Minutes

Total Time: **40** Minutes

INGREDIENTS

- 1 cup whole wheat flour
- ¼ tsp baking soda
- ¼ tsp baking powder
- 2 eggs
- 1 cup milk

DIRECTIONS

1. In a bowl combine all ingredients together and mix well
2. In a skillet heat olive oil
3. Pour ¼ of the batter and cook each pancake for 1-2 minutes per side
4. When ready remove from heat and serve

MUSHROOM OMELETTE

Serves: **1**

Prep Time: **5**   Minutes

Cook Time: **10** Minutes

Total Time: **15** Minutes

INGREDIENTS

- 2 eggs
- ¼ tsp salt
- ¼ tsp black pepper
- 1 tablespoon olive oil
- ¼ cup cheese
- ¼ tsp basil
- 1 cup mushrooms

DIRECTIONS

1. In a bowl combine all ingredients together and mix well
2. In a skillet heat olive oil and pour the egg mixture
3. Cook for 1-2 minutes per side
4. When ready remove omelette from the skillet and serve

OLIVE OMELETTE

Serves: **1**

Prep Time: **5**   Minutes

Cook Time: **10**   Minutes

Total Time: **15**   Minutes

INGREDIENTS

- 2 eggs
- ¼ tsp salt
- ¼ tsp black pepper
- 1 tablespoon olive oil
- ¼ cup cheese
- ½ cup olives
- ¼ tsp basil

DIRECTIONS

1. In a bowl combine all ingredients together and mix well
2. In a skillet heat olive oil and pour the egg mixture
3. Cook for 1-2 minutes per side
4. When ready remove omelette from the skillet and serve

ZUCCHINI OMELETTE

Serves: *1*

Prep Time: *5* Minutes

Cook Time: *10* Minutes

Total Time: *15* Minutes

INGREDIENTS

- 2 eggs
- ¼ tsp salt
- ¼ tsp black pepper
- 1 tablespoon olive oil
- ¼ cup cheese
- ¼ tsp basil
- 1 cup zucchini

DIRECTIONS

1. In a bowl combine all ingredients together and mix well
2. In a skillet heat olive oil and pour the egg mixture
3. Cook for 1-2 minutes per side
4. When ready remove omelette from the skillet and serve

BASIL OMELETTE

Serves: **1**

Prep Time: **5**   Minutes

Cook Time: **10**   Minutes

Total Time: **15**   Minutes

INGREDIENTS

- 2 eggs
- ¼ tsp salt
- ¼ tsp black pepper
- 1 tablespoon olive oil
- ¼ cup cheese
- ¼ tsp basil
- 1 cup red onion

DIRECTIONS

1. In a bowl combine all ingredients together and mix well
2. In a skillet heat olive oil and pour the egg mixture
3. Cook for 1-2 minutes per side
4. When ready remove omelette from the skillet and serve

MUSHROOM OMELETTE

Serves: *1*

Prep Time: *5*   Minutes

Cook Time: *10*   Minutes

Total Time: *15*   Minutes

INGREDIENTS

- 2 eggs
- ¼ tsp salt
- ¼ tsp black pepper
- 1 tablespoon olive oil
- ¼ cup cheese
- ¼ tsp basil
- 1 cup mushrooms

DIRECTIONS

1. In a bowl combine all ingredients together and mix well
2. In a skillet heat olive oil and pour the egg mixture
3. Cook for 1-2 minutes per side
4. When ready remove omelette from the skillet and serve

CHEESE OMELETTE

Serves: **1**

Prep Time: **5**   Minutes

Cook Time: **10** Minutes

Total Time: **15** Minutes

INGREDIENTS

- 2 eggs
- ¼ tsp salt
- ¼ tsp black pepper
- 1 tablespoon olive oil
- ¼ cup cheese
- ¼ tsp basil
- 1 cup tomatoes

DIRECTIONS

1. In a bowl combine all ingredients together and mix well
2. In a skillet heat olive oil and pour the egg mixture
3. Cook for 1-2 minutes per side
4. When ready remove omelette from the skillet and serve

STRAWBERRIES OATMEAL

Serves: 2

Prep Time: 5   Minutes

Cook Time: 10   Minutes

Total Time: 15   Minutes

INGREDIENTS

- 2 cups oats
- 1 cup strawberries
- 1 tablespoon chia seeds
- 1 banana
- 2 cups almond milk
- 1 tablespoon maple syrup

DIRECTIONS

1. Mash banana and strawberries together, set aside
2. In a saucepan add the rest of the ingredients and bring to a boil
3. Reduce heat and cook for 4-5 minutes
4. When ready transfer to the mashed banana mixture and mix well
5. Serve when ready

BANANA OATMEAL

Serves: 2

Prep Time: 5   Minutes

Cook Time: 10   Minutes

Total Time: 15   Minutes

INGREDIENTS

- 1 cup oats
- 2 cup almond milk
- 1 tablespoon maple syrup
- 1 banana
- 1 tsp vanilla extract
- ¼ tsp cinnamon
- 1 tablespoon chia seeds

DIRECTIONS

1. Place all ingredients into a saucepan and bring to a boil
2. Simmer for 5-6 minutes
3. When ready remove from heat
4. Transfer to a bowl, top with walnuts and serve

CHERRY-ALMOND OATMEAL

Serves: **1**

Prep Time: **10**   Minutes

Cook Time: **10**   Minutes

Total Time: **20**   Minutes

INGREDIENTS

- ¼ cup gluten free oats
- ¼ cup water
- ¼ cup almond milk
- 1 banana
- 1 tablespoon brown sugar
- ¼ tsp vanilla extract
- ½ cup cherries
- ¼ cup almonds

DIRECTIONS

1. In a saucepan add oats, water, banana, milk and cook for 4-5 minutes
2. When ready remove from heat and add remaining ingredients
3. Mix well and serve

SPINACH SCRAMBLE

Serves: 2

Prep Time: 10   Minutes

Cook Time: 30   Minutes

Total Time: 40   Minutes

INGREDIENTS

- 1 tablespoon olive oil
- 1 onion
- 1 cup spinach
- 1 avocado
- 4 eggs
- 2 cups cheese
- ¼ tsp salt

DIRECTIONS

1. In a skillet sauté onion until soft
2. In a bowl beat the eggs with salt
3. Add remaining ingredients and mix well
4. Place the mixture into a prepare baking dish
5. Bake at 325 F for 25-30 minutes
6. When ready remove from the oven and serve

Serves: **1**

Prep Time: **5**   Minutes

Cook Time: **5**   Minutes

Total Time: **10**   Minutes

INGREDIENTS

- 1 cup corn cereal
- 1 cup rice cereal
- ¼ cup cocoa cereal
- ¼ cup rice cakes

DIRECTIONS

1. In a bowl combine all ingredients together
2. Serve with milk

SAUSAGE BREAKFAST SANDWICH

Serves: 2

Prep Time: 5   Minutes

Cook Time: 15   Minutes

Total Time: 20   Minutes

INGREDIENTS

- ¼ cup egg substitute
- 1 muffin
- 1 turkey sausage patty
- 1 tablespoon cheddar cheese

DIRECTIONS

1. In a skillet pour egg and cook on low heat
2. Place turkey sausage patty in a pan and cook for 4-5 minutes per side
3. On a toasted muffin place the cooked egg, top with a sausage patty and cheddar cheese
4. Serve when ready

BREAKFAST GRANOLA

Serves: 2

Prep Time: 5   Minutes

Cook Time: 30   Minutes

Total Time: 35   Minutes

INGREDIENTS

- 1 tsp vanilla extract
- 1 tablespoon honey
- 1 lb. rolled oats
- 2 tablespoons sesame seeds
- ¼ lb. almonds
- ¼ lb. berries

DIRECTIONS

1. Preheat the oven to 325 F
2. Spread the granola onto a baking sheet
3. Bake for 12-15 minutes, remove and mix everything
4. Bake for another 12-15 minutes or until slightly brown
5. When ready remove from the oven and serve

PANCAKES

BLUEBERRY PANCAKES

Serves: **4**

Prep Time: **10** Minutes

Cook Time: **20** Minutes

Total Time: **30** Minutes

INGREDIENTS

- 1 cup whole wheat flour
- ¼ tsp baking soda
- ¼ tsp baking powder
- 1 cup blueberries
- 2 eggs
- 1 cup milk

DIRECTIONS

1. In a bowl combine all ingredients together and mix well
2. In a skillet heat olive oil
3. Pour ¼ of the batter and cook each pancake for 1-2 minutes per side
4. When ready remove from heat and serve

PEACH PANCAKES

Serves: **4**

Prep Time: **10** Minutes

Cook Time: **30** Minutes

Total Time: **40** Minutes

INGREDIENTS

- 1 cup whole wheat flour
- ¼ tsp baking soda
- ¼ tsp baking powder
- 1 cup mashed peaches
- 2 eggs
- 1 cup milk

DIRECTIONS

1. In a bowl combine all ingredients together and mix well
2. In a skillet heat olive oil
3. Pour ¼ of the batter and cook each pancake for 1-2 minutes per side
4. When ready remove from heat and serve

BANANA PANCAKES

Serves: **4**

Prep Time: **10**   Minutes

Cook Time: **20**   Minutes

Total Time: **30**   Minutes

INGREDIENTS

- 1 cup whole wheat flour
- ¼ tsp baking soda
- ¼ tsp baking powder
- 1 cup mashed banana
- 2 eggs
- 1 cup milk

DIRECTIONS

1. In a bowl combine all ingredients together and mix well
2. In a skillet heat olive oil
3. Pour ¼ of the batter and cook each pancake for 1-2 minutes per side
4. When ready remove from heat and serve

PLUMS PANCAKES

Serves: **4**

Prep Time: **10**   Minutes

Cook Time: **20**   Minutes

Total Time: **30**   Minutes

INGREDIENTS

- 1 cup whole wheat flour
- ¼ tsp baking soda
- ¼ tsp baking powder
- 1 cup mashed plums
- 2 eggs
- 1 cup milk

DIRECTIONS

1. In a bowl combine all ingredients together and mix well
2. In a skillet heat olive oil
3. Pour ¼ of the batter and cook each pancake for 1-2 minutes per side
4. When ready remove from heat and serve

PANCAKES

Serves: **4**

Prep Time: **10** Minutes

Cook Time: **30** Minutes

Total Time: **40** Minutes

INGREDIENTS

- 1 cup whole wheat flour
- ¼ tsp baking soda
- ¼ tsp baking powder
- 2 eggs
- 1 cup milk

DIRECTIONS

1. In a bowl combine all ingredients together and mix well
2. In a skillet heat olive oil
3. Pour ¼ of the batter and cook each pancake for 1-2 minutes per side
4. When ready remove from heat and serve

COOKIES

BREAKFAST COOKIES

Serves: *8-12*

Prep Time: 5   Minutes

Cook Time: *15*   Minutes

Total Time: *20*   Minutes

INGREDIENTS

- 1 cup rolled oats
- ¼ cup applesauce
- ½ tsp vanilla extract
- 3 tablespoons chocolate chips
- 2 tablespoons dried fruits
- 1 tsp cinnamon

DIRECTIONS

1. Preheat the oven to 325 F
2. In a bowl combine all ingredients together and mix well
3. Scoop cookies using an ice cream scoop
4. Place cookies onto a prepared baking sheet
5. Place in the oven for 12-15 minutes or until the cookies are done
6. When ready remove from the oven and serve

CLEMENTINE SMOOTHIE

Serves: **1**

Prep Time: **5**   Minutes

Cook Time: **5**   Minutes

Total Time: **10**   Minutes

INGREDIENTS

- 4 oz. clementine juice
- 2 oz. oats
- 2 oz. blueberries
- 2 pears
- 1 tablespoon honey
- 1 tsp mixed spice

DIRECTIONS

1. In a blender place all ingredients and blend until smooth
2. Pour smoothie in a glass and serve

AVOCADO SMOOTHIE

Serves: *1*
Prep Time: 5   Minutes

Cook Time: 5   Minutes

Total Time: *10*   Minutes

INGREDIENTS

- 1 banana
- 2 tablespoons cacao powder
- 1 tsp coconut oil
- 1 avocado
- 1 tsp vanilla extract
- 2 tablespoons honey
- 1 cup ice

DIRECTIONS

1. In a blender place all ingredients and blend until smooth
2. Pour smoothie in a glass and serve

PEAR SMOOTHIE

Serves: **1**

Prep Time: **5**   Minutes

Cook Time: **5**   Minutes

Total Time: **10** Minutes

INGREDIENTS

- 2 pears
- 1 banana
- 1 cup almond milk
- ½ cup vanilla yoghurt
- 1 tsp cinnamon

DIRECTIONS

1. In a blender place all ingredients and blend until smooth
2. Pour smoothie in a glass and serve

Serves: *1*

Prep Time: *5*   Minutes

Cook Time: *5*   Minutes

Total Time: *10* Minutes

INGREDIENTS

- 1 banana
- 1 tsp coffee
- 1 tsp cinnamon
- 1 tsp honey
- 1 cup milk

DIRECTIONS

1. In a blender place all ingredients and blend until smooth
2. Pour smoothie in a glass and serve

BANANA SMOOTHIE

Serves: *1*
Prep Time: *5*   Minutes

Cook Time: *5*   Minutes

Total Time: *10*   Minutes

INGREDIENTS

- 2 tablespoons cocoa powder
- 1 cup ice
- 1 banana
- 1 cup skimmed milk

DIRECTIONS

1. In a blender place all ingredients and blend until smooth
2. Pour smoothie in a glass and serve

GREEN SMOOTHIE

Serves: *1*

Prep Time: *5*   Minutes

Cook Time: *5*   Minutes

Total Time: *10*   Minutes

INGREDIENTS

- 1 banana
- 1 apple
- 1 kiwi
- 2 oz. spinach

DIRECTIONS

1. In a blender place all ingredients and blend until smooth
2. Pour smoothie in a glass and serve

KALE SMOOTHIE

Serves: *1*

Prep Time: *5*   Minutes

Cook Time: *5*   Minutes

Total Time: *10* Minutes

INGREDIENTS

- 2 oz. spinach leaves
- 1 cup soy milk
- 1 tablespoon peanut butter
- 1 tablespoon chia seeds
- 1 banana

DIRECTIONS

1. In a blender place all ingredients and blend until smooth
2. Pour smoothie in a glass and serve

GREEN JUICE SMOOTHIE

Serves: *1*

Prep Time: 5   Minutes

Cook Time: 5   Minutes

Total Time: *10*   Minutes

INGREDIENTS

- 2 apples
- 2 celery sticks
- 1 cucumber
- ½ cup kale leaves
- ¼ lemon

DIRECTIONS

1. In a blender place all ingredients and blend until smooth
2. Pour smoothie in a glass and serve

SPICY SMOOTHIE

Serves: **1**

Prep Time: **5**   Minutes

Cook Time: **5**   Minutes

Total Time: **10**   Minutes

INGREDIENTS

- 1 banana
- 2 oz. baby spinach
- 1 cup mango
- ¼ tsp jalapeno pepper
- 1 cup water

DIRECTIONS

1. In a blender place all ingredients and blend until smooth
2. Pour smoothie in a glass and serve

COCONUT SMOOTHIE

Serves: *1*

Prep Time: *5*   Minutes

Cook Time: *5*   Minutes

Total Time: *10* Minutes

INGREDIENTS

- 1 mango
- 1 banana
- 1 cup coconut milk
- 1 cup pineapple chunks
- 2 tablespoons coconut flakes

DIRECTIONS

1. In a blender place all ingredients and blend until smooth
2. Pour smoothie in a glass and serve

MUFFINS

SIMPLE MUFFINS

Serves: *8-12*

Prep Time: *10*   Minutes

Cook Time: *20*   Minutes

Total Time: *30*   Minutes

INGREDIENTS

- 2 eggs
- 1 tablespoon olive oil
- 1 cup milk
- 2 cups whole wheat flour
- 1 tsp baking soda
- ¼ tsp baking soda
- 1 cup pumpkin puree
- 1 tsp cinnamon
- ¼ cup molasses

DIRECTIONS

1. In a bowl combine all wet ingredients
2. In another bowl combine all dry ingredients
3. Combine wet and dry ingredients together
4. Pour mixture into 8-12 prepared muffin cups, fill 2/3 of the cups

5. Bake for 18-20 minutes at 375 F

6. When ready remove from the oven and serve

GINGERBREAD MUFFINS

Serves: **8-12**

Prep Time: **10**   Minutes

Cook Time: **20**   Minutes

Total Time: **30**   Minutes

INGREDIENTS

- 2 eggs
- 1 tablespoon olive oil
- 1 cup milk
- 2 cups whole wheat flour
- 1 tsp baking soda
- ¼ tsp baking soda
- 1 tsp ginger
- 1 tsp cinnamon
- ¼ cup molasses

DIRECTIONS

1. In a bowl combine all wet ingredients
2. In another bowl combine all dry ingredients
3. Combine wet and dry ingredients together
4. Fold in ginger and mix well
5. Pour mixture into 8-12 prepared muffin cups, fill 2/3 of the cups

6. Bake for 18-20 minutes at 375 F
7. When ready remove from the oven and serve

KIWI MUFFINS

Serves: *8-12*

Prep Time: *10*   Minutes

Cook Time: *20*   Minutes

Total Time: *30*   Minutes

INGREDIENTS

- 2 eggs
- 1 tablespoon olive oil
- 1 cup milk
- 2 cups whole wheat flour
- 1 tsp baking soda
- ¼ tsp baking soda
- 1 tsp cinnamon
- 1 cup mashed kiwi

DIRECTIONS

1. In a bowl combine all wet ingredients
2. In another bowl combine all dry ingredients
3. Combine wet and dry ingredients together
4. Pour mixture into 8-12 prepared muffin cups, fill 2/3 of the cups
5. Bake for 18-20 minutes at 375 F
6. When ready remove from the oven and serve

BLUEBERRY MUFFINS

Serves: *8-12*

Prep Time: *10*   Minutes

Cook Time: *20*   Minutes

Total Time: *30*   Minutes

INGREDIENTS

- 2 eggs
- 1 tablespoon olive oil
- 1 cup milk
- 2 cups whole wheat flour
- 1 tsp baking soda
- ¼ tsp baking soda
- 1 tsp cinnamon
- 1 cup blueberries

DIRECTIONS

1. In a bowl combine all wet ingredients
2. In another bowl combine all dry ingredients
3. Combine wet and dry ingredients together
4. Pour mixture into 8-12 prepared muffin cups, fill 2/3 of the cups
5. Bake for 18-20 minutes at 375 F
6. When ready remove from the oven and serve

PLUM MUFFINS

Serves: *8-12*

Prep Time: *10*   Minutes

Cook Time: *20*   Minutes

Total Time: *30*   Minutes

INGREDIENTS

- 2 eggs
- 1 tablespoon olive oil
- 1 cup milk
- 2 cups whole wheat flour
- 1 tsp baking soda
- ¼ tsp baking soda
- 1 tsp cinnamon
- 1 cup mashed plums

DIRECTIONS

1. In a bowl combine all wet ingredients
2. In another bowl combine all dry ingredients
3. Combine wet and dry ingredients together
4. Pour mixture into 8-12 prepared muffin cups, fill 2/3 of the cups
5. Bake for 18-20 minutes at 375 F
6. When ready remove from the oven and serve

CHOCOLATE MUFFINS

Serves: *8-12*

Prep Time: *10*   Minutes

Cook Time: *20*   Minutes

Total Time: *30*   Minutes

INGREDIENTS

- 2 eggs
- 1 tablespoon olive oil
- 1 cup milk
- 2 cups whole wheat flour
- 1 tsp baking soda
- ¼ tsp baking soda
- 1 tsp cinnamon
- 1 cup chocolate chips

DIRECTIONS

1. In a bowl combine all wet ingredients
2. In another bowl combine all dry ingredients
3. Combine wet and dry ingredients together
4. Fold in chocolate chips and mix well
5. Pour mixture into 8-12 prepared muffin cups, fill 2/3 of the cups
6. Bake for 18-20 minutes at 375 F

PRUNES MUFFINS

Serves: **8-12**

Prep Time: **10**   Minutes

Cook Time: **20**   Minutes

Total Time: **30**   Minutes

INGREDIENTS

- 2 eggs
- 1 tablespoon olive oil
- 1 cup milk
- 2 cups whole wheat flour
- 1 tsp baking soda
- 1 cup mashed prunes
- ¼ tsp baking soda
- 1 tsp cinnamon
- 1 cup mashed prunes

DIRECTIONS

1. In a bowl combine all wet ingredients
2. In another bowl combine all dry ingredients
3. Combine wet and dry ingredients together
4. Pour mixture into 8-12 prepared muffin cups, fill 2/3 of the cups
5. Bake for 18-20 minutes at 375 F

THIRD COOKBOOK

CHOCOLATE COCONUT OATS

Serves: **4**

Prep Time: **10** Minutes

Cook Time: **10** Minutes

Total Time: **20** Minutes

INGREDIENTS

- 1 cup oats
- 2 tablespoons chia seeds
- 2 tablespoons maple syrup
- 1 vanilla extract
- 1 tablespoon cocoa powder
- 1 cup water
- 2/3 cup coconut milk
- 2 tablespoons water

DIRECTIONS

1. In a bowl mix oat with water and place it in the fridge overnight
2. In the morning add chia seeds and coconut milk
3. Transfer mixture to a skillet and cook for 5 minutes
4. Remove and move into serving bowl and add vanilla extract, cacao powder and maple syrup

QUINOA MUESLY WITH COCONUT MILK

Serves: **4**

Prep Time: **10**   Minutes

Cook Time: **10**   Minutes

Total Time: **20**   Minutes

INGREDIENTS

- 1 cup Quinoa
- ½ cup coconut milk yogurt
- 1 pinch ground cinnamon
- 1 cup Grain Free Muesli

DIRECTIONS

1. Cook the quinoa according to the indications, nd set aside
2. Drizzle the quinoa with coconut milk yogurt and top with grain free muesli
3. Add cinnamon to each bowl and serve

SWEET POTATO

Serves: **4**

Prep Time: **10** Minutes

Cook Time: **30** Minutes

Total Time: **40** Minutes

INGREDIENTS

- 3 sweet potatoes
- 8 tablespoons almond milk
- 1 tablespoon mint leaves
- 1 tablespoon lemon zest
- 1 tablespoon coconut oil
- 1 pinch salt
- 1 pinch ground cinnamon
- 3 tablespoons vanilla cereal

DIRECTIONS

1. Preheat oven to 350 F and line a baking sheet with parchment paper
2. Place the sweet potatoes on the baking sheet
3. Rub the sweet potato with coconut oil and sprinkle salt and pepper
4. Roast for 30 minutes

5. Remove the sweet potatoes from the oven and cut into small pieces

6. Top with coconut oil, lemon zest and cereal mixture

BANANA SPLIT

Serves: **2**

Prep Time: **10** Minutes

Cook Time: **10** Minutes

Total Time: **20** Minutes

INGREDIENTS

- 2 bananas
- 1 cup strawberries
- 1 cup blackberries
- 1 cup chopped pineapple
- 1 cup coconut milk
- 1 tablespoon whole grain granola
- ¼ ounce roasted coconut chips

DIRECTIONS

1. Slice the bananas and place them into a bowl
2. Divide the strawberries, blackberries and pineapple and place it in the bottom of the bowl
3. Top with yogurt and divide the granola and coconut chips between the bananas

Serves: **2**

Prep Time: **10** Minutes

Cook Time: **30** Minutes

Total Time: **40** Minutes

INGREDIENTS

- 1 cup oats
- ½ tsp ground cinnamon
- 1 tsp maple syrup
- 1 tablespoon walnut halves
- 2 tsp coconut oil
- 1 Anjou pear spiralized with blade
- 1 cup almond milk
- ½ tsp vanilla extract

DIRECTIONS

1. In a saucepan boil water and add oats for another 10 minutes
2. In a skillet heat coconut oil over medium heat and add almond milk, pear noodles, cinnamon, maple syrup and vanilla extract
3. Stir to simmer for about 10-15 minutes
4. In another skillet place walnuts and cook for 5-6 minutes, remove from pan when ready

5. Place the oatmeal in a bowl and top with pear mixture and toasted walnuts

CHOCOLATE BREAD

Serves: 2

Prep Time: **10**   Minutes

Cook Time: **30**   Minutes

Total Time: **40**   Minutes

INGREDIENTS

- Coconut oil
- 1 cup oat flour
- ½ cup almond flour
- 1 tablespoon flaxseeds
- 5 tablespoons water
- ½ cup almond milk
- 1 tsp baking powder
- 1 tsp baking soda
- 1 tsp vanilla extract
- ½ cup maple syrup
- 1 banana
- ½ cup cocoa powder

DIRECTIONS

1. Preheat oven to 300 F
2. Mix water with flax and water and set aside

3. In a bowl mash the banana and add remaining ingredients
4. Transfer the mixture to a loaf pan and bake for 40 minutes
5. Remove from the oven and let it cool
6. Slice the bread and serve

COCONUT CRACKERS

Serves: 2

Prep Time: **10**   Minutes

Cook Time: **60**   Minutes

Total Time: **70**   Minutes

INGREDIENTS

- 1 cup hazelnut flour
- 1 peach
- 8 tablespoons water
- 6 tablespoons olive oil
- ¾ tsp salt
- 1 tsp cacao powder
- ½ tsp cinnamon
- 1 cup water
- ¼ tsp ginger
- ½ tablespoons coconut flakes
- 1 cup coconut flour
- 2 tablespoons flaxseeds
- 1 tablespoon cherries

DIRECTIONS

1. Preheat oven to 325 F

2. In a bowl mix water with flaxseeds

3. In another bowl mix all the ingredients, excepting coconut flakes and form a ball

4. Transfer the dough to a baking sheet with parchment paper

5. Sprinkle with coconut flakes and bake for 50 minutes

6. Remove and let it cool before serving

ALMOND BUTTER

Serves: **4**

Prep Time: **10**   Minutes

Cook Time: **30**   Minutes

Total Time: **40**   Minutes

INGREDIENTS

- 1 cup pitted dates
- 2 bananas
- 1 cup almond flour
- 1 cup oats
- 2 tablespoons almond butter
- 2 tablespoons cherries
- 1 tsp sesame seeds

DIRECTIONS

1. In a food processor puree the dates until well combined
2. Add bananas and puree them also
3. Add oats, almond butter, almond flour, and puree until well combined
4. Transfer to the fridge for 25-30 minutes
5. Remove from fridge and add cherries and mix and also sesame seeds

6. Roll into small balls and place them on a baking sheet and bake for 20-25 minutes

7. Remove from oven and let them cool before serving

Serves: **1**

Prep Time: **5** Minutes

Cook Time: **5** Minutes

Total Time: **10** Minutes

INGREDIENTS

- ½ cup dried raisins
- ½ cup dried pecans
- ¼ cup almonds
- 1 cup coconut milk
- 1 tsp cinnamon

DIRECTIONS

3. In a bowl combine all ingredients together
4. Serve with milk

CRANBERRY BREAKFAST MIX

Serves: **1**

Prep Time: **5** Minutes

Cook Time: **5** Minutes

Total Time: **10** Minutes

INGREDIENTS

- ½ cup cranberries
- ½ cup dried pecans
- ¼ cup oats
- 1 tablespoon corn cereal
- 1 tsp cinnamon

DIRECTIONS

1. In a bowl combine all ingredients together
2. Serve with milk

BREAKFAST MIX

Serves: **1**

Prep Time: **5** Minutes

Cook Time: **5** Minutes

Total Time: **10** Minutes

INGREDIENTS

- 1 cup oats
- 1 cup mix dried fruits
- 1 tsp cinnamon
- 1 cup coconut milk

DIRECTIONS

1. In a bowl combine all ingredients together
2. Serve with milk

ACAI PANCAKES

Serves: **4**

Prep Time: **10** Minutes

Cook Time: **20** Minutes

Total Time: **30** Minutes

INGREDIENTS

- 1 cup whole wheat flour
- ¼ tsp baking soda
- ¼ tsp baking powder
- 1 cup acai
- 2 eggs
- 1 cup milk

DIRECTIONS

1. In a bowl combine all ingredients together and mix well
2. In a skillet heat olive oil
3. Pour ¼ of the batter and cook each pancake for 1-2 minutes per side
4. When ready remove from heat and serve

AKEE PANCAKES

Serves: **4**

Prep Time: **10** Minutes

Cook Time: **30** Minutes

Total Time: **40** Minutes

INGREDIENTS

- 1 cup whole wheat flour
- ¼ tsp baking soda
- ¼ tsp baking powder
- 1 cup akee
- 2 eggs
- 1 cup milk

DIRECTIONS

1. In a bowl combine all ingredients together and mix well
2. In a skillet heat olive oil
3. Pour ¼ of the batter and cook each pancake for 1-2 minutes per side
4. When ready remove from heat and serve

APPLE PANCAKES

Serves: **4**

Prep Time: **10** Minutes

Cook Time: **20** Minutes

Total Time: **30** Minutes

INGREDIENTS

- 1 cup whole wheat flour
- ¼ tsp baking soda
- ¼ tsp baking powder
- 1 cup mashed apple
- 2 eggs
- 1 cup milk

DIRECTIONS

1. In a bowl combine all ingredients together and mix well
2. In a skillet heat olive oil
3. Pour ¼ of the batter and cook each pancake for 1-2 minutes per side
4. When ready remove from heat and serve

AVOCADO PANCAKES

Serves: **4**

Prep Time: **10** Minutes

Cook Time: **20** Minutes

Total Time: **30** Minutes

INGREDIENTS

- 1 cup whole wheat flour
- ¼ tsp baking soda
- ¼ tsp baking powder
- 1 cup avocado
- 2 eggs
- 1 cup milk

DIRECTIONS

1. In a bowl combine all ingredients together and mix well
2. In a skillet heat olive oil
3. Pour ¼ of the batter and cook each pancake for 1-2 minutes per side
4. When ready remove from heat and serve

SIMPLE PANCAKES

Serves: **4**

Prep Time: **10** Minutes

Cook Time: **30** Minutes

Total Time: **40** Minutes

INGREDIENTS

- 1 cup whole wheat flour
- ¼ tsp baking soda
- ¼ tsp baking powder
- 2 eggs
- 1 cup milk

DIRECTIONS

1. In a bowl combine all ingredients together and mix well
2. In a skillet heat olive oil
3. Pour ¼ of the batter and cook each pancake for 1-2 minutes per side
4. When ready remove from heat and serve

GINGERBREAD MUFFINS

Serves: *8-12*

Prep Time: *10*   Minutes

Cook Time: *20*   Minutes

Total Time: *30*   Minutes

INGREDIENTS

- 2 eggs
- 1 tablespoon olive oil
- 1 cup milk
- 2 cups whole wheat flour
- 1 tsp baking soda
- ¼ tsp baking soda
- 1 tsp ginger
- 1 tsp cinnamon
- ¼ cup molasses

DIRECTIONS

1. In a bowl combine all wet ingredients
2. In another bowl combine all dry ingredients
3. Combine wet and dry ingredients together
4. Pour mixture into 8-12 prepared muffin cups, fill 2/3 of the cups
5. Bake for 18-20 minutes at 375 F, when ready remove and serve

BLACKBERRY MUFFINS

Serves: *8-12*

Prep Time: *10*   Minutes

Cook Time: *20*   Minutes

Total Time: *30*   Minutes

INGREDIENTS

- 2 eggs
- 1 tablespoon olive oil
- 1 cup milk
- 2 cups whole wheat flour
- 1 tsp baking soda
- ¼ tsp baking soda
- 1 tsp cinnamon
- 1 cup blackberry

DIRECTIONS

1. In a bowl combine all wet ingredients
2. In another bowl combine all dry ingredients
3. Combine wet and dry ingredients together
4. Pour mixture into 8-12 prepared muffin cups, fill 2/3 of the cups
5. Bake for 18-20 minutes at 375 F
6. When ready remove from the oven and serve

CHERRY MUFFINS

Serves: *8-12*

Prep Time: *10*   Minutes

Cook Time: *20*   Minutes

Total Time: *30*   Minutes

INGREDIENTS

- 2 eggs
- 1 tablespoon olive oil
- 1 cup milk
- 2 cups whole wheat flour
- 1 tsp baking soda
- ¼ tsp baking soda
- 1 tsp cinnamon
- 1 cup cherries

DIRECTIONS

1. In a bowl combine all wet ingredients
2. In another bowl combine all dry ingredients
3. Combine wet and dry ingredients together
4. Pour mixture into 8-12 prepared muffin cups, fill 2/3 of the cups
5. Bake for 18-20 minutes at 375 F
6. When ready remove from the oven and serve

COCONUT MUFFINS

Serves: *8-12*

Prep Time: *10*   Minutes

Cook Time: *20*   Minutes

Total Time: *30*   Minutes

INGREDIENTS

- 2 eggs
- 1 tablespoon olive oil
- 1 cup milk
- 2 cups whole wheat flour
- 1 tsp baking soda
- ¼ tsp baking soda
- 1 tsp cinnamon
- 1 cup coconut flakes

DIRECTIONS

1. In a bowl combine all wet ingredients
2. In another bowl combine all dry ingredients
3. Combine wet and dry ingredients together
4. Pour mixture into 8-12 prepared muffin cups, fill 2/3 of the cups
5. Bake for 18-20 minutes at 375 F
6. When ready remove from the oven and serve

CHOCOLATE MUFFINS

Serves: *8-12*

Prep Time: *10*   Minutes

Cook Time: *20*   Minutes

Total Time: *30*   Minutes

INGREDIENTS

- 2 eggs
- 1 tablespoon olive oil
- 1 cup milk
- 2 cups whole wheat flour
- 1 tsp baking soda
- ¼ tsp baking soda
- 1 tsp cinnamon
- 1 cup chocolate chips

DIRECTIONS

1. In a bowl combine all wet ingredients
2. In another bowl combine all dry ingredients
3. Combine wet and dry ingredients together
4. Pour mixture into 8-12 prepared muffin cups, fill 2/3 of the cups
5. Bake for 18-20 minutes at 375 F
6. When ready remove from the oven and serve

RAISIN MUFFINS

Serves: *8-12*

Prep Time: **10**   Minutes

Cook Time: **20**   Minutes

Total Time: **30**   Minutes

INGREDIENTS

- 2 eggs
- 1 tablespoon olive oil
- 1 cup milk
- 2 cups whole wheat flour
- 1 tsp baking soda
- ¼ tsp baking soda
- 1 tsp cinnamon
- 1 cup dates

DIRECTIONS

1. In a bowl combine all wet ingredients
2. In another bowl combine all dry ingredients
3. Combine wet and dry ingredients together
4. Pour mixture into 8-12 prepared muffin cups, fill 2/3 of the cups
5. Bake for 18-20 minutes at 375 F
6. When ready remove from the oven and serve

SIMPLE OMELETTE

Serves: *1*
Prep Time: *5*   Minutes

Cook Time: *10* Minutes

Total Time: *15* Minutes

INGREDIENTS

- 2 eggs
- ¼ tsp salt
- ¼ tsp black pepper
- 1 tablespoon olive oil
- ¼ cup cheese
- ¼ tsp basil

DIRECTIONS

1. In a bowl combine all ingredients together and mix well
2. In a skillet heat olive oil and pour the egg mixture
3. Cook for 1-2 minutes per side
4. When ready remove omelette from the skillet and serve

ASPARAGUS OMELETTE

Serves: **1**

Prep Time: **5**   Minutes

Cook Time: **10** Minutes

Total Time: **15** Minutes

INGREDIENTS

- 2 eggs
- ¼ tsp salt
- ¼ tsp black pepper
- 1 tablespoon olive oil
- ¼ cup cheese
- ¼ tsp basil
- 1 cup asparagus

DIRECTIONS

1. In a bowl combine all ingredients together and mix well
2. In a skillet heat olive oil and pour the egg mixture
3. Cook for 1-2 minutes per side
4. When ready remove omelette from the skillet and serve

BLACK BEANS OMELETTE

Serves: **1**

Prep Time: **5**   Minutes

Cook Time: **10**   Minutes

Total Time: **15**   Minutes

INGREDIENTS

- 2 eggs
- ¼ tsp salt
- ¼ tsp black pepper
- 1 tablespoon olive oil
- ¼ cup cheese
- ¼ tsp basil
- 1 cup red onion
- 1 cup black beans

DIRECTIONS

1. In a bowl combine all ingredients together and mix well
2. In a skillet heat olive oil and pour the egg mixture
3. Cook for 1-2 minutes per side
4. When ready remove omelette from the skillet and serve

LENTIL OMELETTE

Serves: **1**

Prep Time: **5**   Minutes

Cook Time: **10**   Minutes

Total Time: **15**   Minutes

INGREDIENTS

- 2 eggs
- ¼ tsp salt
- ¼ tsp black pepper
- 1 tablespoon olive oil
- ¼ cup cheese
- ¼ tsp basil
- 1 cup lentils

DIRECTIONS

1. In a bowl combine all ingredients together and mix well
2. In a skillet heat olive oil and pour the egg mixture
3. Cook for 1-2 minutes per side
4. When ready remove omelette from the skillet and serve

ENDIVE OMELETTE

Serves: **1**

Prep Time: **5**   Minutes

Cook Time: **10**   Minutes

Total Time: **15**   Minutes

INGREDIENTS

- 2 eggs
- ¼ tsp salt
- ¼ tsp black pepper
- 1 tablespoon olive oil
- ¼ cup cheese
- ¼ tsp basil
- 1 cup endive

DIRECTIONS

1. In a bowl combine all ingredients together and mix well
2. In a skillet heat olive oil and pour the egg mixture
3. Cook for 1-2 minutes per side
4. When ready remove omelette from the skillet and serve

TART RECIPES

PEAR TART

Serves: **6-8**

Prep Time: **25**   Minutes

Cook Time: **25**   Minutes

Total Time: **50**   Minutes

INGREDIENTS

- 1 lb. pears
- 2 oz. brown sugar
- ½ lb. flaked almonds
- ¼ lb. porridge oat
- 2 oz. flour
- ¼ lb. almonds
- pastry sheets
- 2 tablespoons syrup

DIRECTIONS

1. Preheat oven to 400 F, unfold pastry sheets and place them on a baking sheet
2. Toss together all ingredients together and mix well
3. Spread mixture in a single layer on the pastry sheets
4. Before baking decorate with your desired fruits

5. Bake at 400 F for 22-25 minutes or until golden brown

6. When ready remove from the oven and serve

CARDAMOM TART

Serves: **6-8**

Prep Time: **25**   Minutes

Cook Time: **25**   Minutes

Total Time: **50**   Minutes

INGREDIENTS

- 4-5 pears
- 2 tablespoons lemon juice
- pastry sheets

CARDAMOMO FILLING

- ½ lb. butter
- ½ lb. brown sugar
- ½ lb. almonds
- ¼ lb. flour
- 1 ¼ tsp cardamom
- 2 eggs

DIRECTIONS

1. Preheat oven to 400 F, unfold pastry sheets and place them on a baking sheet
2. Toss together all ingredients together and mix well
3. Spread mixture in a single layer on the pastry sheets
4. Before baking decorate with your desired fruits

5. Bake at 400 F for 22-25 minutes or until golden brown

6. When ready remove from the oven and serve

PEACH PECAN PIE

Serves: *8-12*

Prep Time: *15*   Minutes

Cook Time: *35*   Minutes

Total Time: *50*   Minutes

INGREDIENTS

- 4-5 cups peaches
- 1 tablespoon preserves
- 1 cup sugar
- 4 small egg yolks
- ¼ cup flour
- 1 tsp vanilla extract

DIRECTIONS

1. Line a pie plate or pie form with pastry and cover the edges of the plate depending on your preference
2. In a bowl combine all pie ingredients together and mix well
3. Pour the mixture over the pastry
4. Bake at 400-425 F for 25-30 minutes or until golden brown
5. When ready remove from the oven and let it rest for 15 minutes

BUTTERFINGER PIE

Serves: *8-12*

Prep Time: *15*   Minutes

Cook Time: *35*   Minutes

Total Time: *50*   Minutes

INGREDIENTS

- pastry sheets
- 1 package cream cheese
- 1 tsp vanilla extract
- ¼ cup peanut butter
- 1 cup powdered sugar (to decorate)
- 2 cups Butterfinger candy bars
- 8 oz whipped topping

DIRECTIONS

1. Line a pie plate or pie form with pastry and cover the edges of the plate depending on your preference
2. In a bowl combine all pie ingredients together and mix well
3. Pour the mixture over the pastry
4. Bake at 400-425 F for 25-30 minutes or until golden brown
5. When ready remove from the oven and let it rest for 15 minutes

STRAWBERRY PIE

Serves: *8-12*

Prep Time: *15*   Minutes

Cook Time: *35*   Minutes

Total Time: *50*   Minutes

INGREDIENTS

- pastry sheets
- 1,5 lb. strawberries
- 1 cup powdered sugar
- 2 tablespoons cornstarch
- 1 tablespoon lime juice
- 1 tsp vanilla extract
- 2 eggs
- 2 tablespoons butter

DIRECTIONS

1. Line a pie plate or pie form with pastry and cover the edges of the plate depending on your preference
2. In a bowl combine all pie ingredients together and mix well
3. Pour the mixture over the pastry
4. Bake at 400-425 F for 25-30 minutes or until golden brown
5. When ready remove from the oven and let it rest for 15 minutes

APPLE-GINGER SMOOTHIE

Serves: *1*

Prep Time: *5*   Minutes

Cook Time: *5*   Minutes

Total Time: *10* Minutes

INGREDIENTS

- 1 apple
- 1 cup almond milk
- 1 cup kale
- 1 tsp ginger

DIRECTIONS

1. In a blender place all ingredients and blend until smooth
2. Pour smoothie in a glass and serve

POMEGRANATE SMOOTHIE

Serves: **1**

Prep Time: **5**   Minutes

Cook Time: **5**   Minutes

Total Time: **10**   Minutes

INGREDIENTS

- 1 cucumber
- 1 pomegranate
- 1 cup ice
- 1 cup almond milk

DIRECTIONS

1. In a blender place all ingredients and blend until smooth
2. Pour smoothie in a glass and serve

MANGO MORNING SMOOTHIE

Serves: *1*
Prep Time: *5*   Minutes

Cook Time: *5*   Minutes

Total Time: *10* Minutes

INGREDIENTS

- 1 mango
- 1 cup strawberries
- 1 cup coconut milk
- 1 cup ice

DIRECTIONS

1. In a blender place all ingredients and blend until smooth
2. Pour smoothie in a glass and serve

CARAMEL SMOOTHIE

Serves: **1**

Prep Time: **5** Minutes

Cook Time: **5** Minutes

Total Time: **10** Minutes

INGREDIENTS

- 1 cup caramel powder
- 1 cup almond milk
- 1 tsp cinnamon

DIRECTIONS

1. In a blender place all ingredients and blend until smooth
2. Pour smoothie in a glass and serve

BASIL SMOOTHIE

Serves: **1**

Prep Time: **5** Minutes

Cook Time: **5** Minutes

Total Time: **10** Minutes

INGREDIENTS

- 1 cup blueberries
- 1 cup water
- 2 basil leaves
- ½ cup coconut milk
- 1 tablespoon peanut butter

DIRECTIONS

1. In a blender place all ingredients and blend until smooth
2. Pour smoothie in a glass and serve

PROTEIN SMOOTHIE

Serves: **1**

Prep Time: **5**   Minutes

Cook Time: **5**   Minutes

Total Time: **10** Minutes

INGREDIENTS

- 1 cup blueberries
- 1 cup cauliflower
- 1 cup vanilla yoghurt
- 1 cup protein powder

DIRECTIONS

1. In a blender place all ingredients and blend until smooth
2. Pour smoothie in a glass and serve

Serves: *1*

Prep Time: *5*   Minutes

Cook Time: *5*   Minutes

Total Time: *10* Minutes

INGREDIENTS

- 1 nectarine
- 2 oz. cauliflower
- 2 oz. swiss chard
- 1 tablespoon almond butter

DIRECTIONS

1. In a blender place all ingredients and blend until smooth
2. Pour smoothie in a glass and serve

ICE-CREAM RECIPES

PISTACHIOS ICE-CREAM

Serves: **6-8**

Prep Time: **15** Minutes

Cook Time: **15** Minutes

Total Time: **30** Minutes

INGREDIENTS

- 4 egg yolks
- 1 cup heavy cream
- 1 cup milk
- 1 cup sugar
- 1 vanilla bean
- 1 tsp almond extract
- 1 cup cherries
- ½ cup pistachios

DIRECTIONS

1. In a saucepan whisk together all ingredients
2. Mix until bubbly
3. Strain into a bowl and cool
4. Whisk in favorite fruits and mix well
5. Cover and refrigerate for 2-3 hours

6. Pour mixture in the ice-cream maker and follow manufacturer instructions

7. Serve when ready

VANILLA ICE-CREAM

Serves: **6-8**

Prep Time: **15**   Minutes
Cook Time: **15**   Minutes
Total Time: **30**   Minutes

INGREDIENTS

- 1 cup milk
- 1 tablespoon cornstarch
- 1 oz. cream cheese
- 1 cup heavy cream
- 1 cup brown sugar
- 1 tablespoon corn syrup
- 1 vanilla bean

DIRECTIONS

1. In a saucepan whisk together all ingredients
2. Mix until bubbly
3. Strain into a bowl and cool
4. Whisk in favorite fruits and mix well
5. Cover and refrigerate for 2-3 hours
6. Pour mixture in the ice-cream maker and follow manufacturer instructions
7. Serve when ready

FOURTH COOKBOOK

SIDE DISHES

QUINOA FALAFEL

Serves: **6-8**

Prep Time: **15**   Minutes

Cook Time: **25**   Minutes

Total Time: **40**   Minutes

INGREDIENTS

- 2 cups cooked quinoa
- 2 cups chickpeas
- 1 onion
- 1 tablespoon tahini
- 4 garlic cloves
- 1 cup parsley
- 2 tsp cumin
- 1 tsp coriander
- 2 tablespoons olive oil
- 1 tablespoon lemon juice

TAHINI SAUCE

- 1 cup water
- 1 cup tahini
- 1 garlic clove
- pinch of salt

159

DIRECTIONS

1. In a blender add garlic, parsley, coriander, lemon juice, onion and blend until smooth
2. Add the remaining ingredients and blend again
3. Form patties and freeze patties for 15-20 minutes
4. In a frying pan place the patties and fry until golden brown
5. When ready transfer patties to a plate and serve with tahini sauce

VEGAN RAMEN

Serves: **6**

Prep Time: **10**   Minutes

Cook Time: **20**   Minutes

Total Time: **30**   Minutes

INGREDIENTS

- 4 cups vegetable broth
- 2 tablespoon soy sauce
- 2 clove garlic
- 1 tsp miso paste
- 1 cup mushrooms
- 1 cup tofu
- 1 cup broccoli florets
- 1 cup ramen noodles
- 1 cup sprouts
- ½ red onion
- ¼ cup cilantro
- 1 tablespoon sesame seeds

DIRECTIONS

1. In a pan sauté garlic, onion and set aside
2. In a pot add broth and sautéed onion, garlic and stir in miso paste

3. Transfer everything to a blender and blend until smooth
4. Add salt soy sauce and blend again
5. In a pan fry mushrooms, noodles, broccoli, sprouts, and tofu
6. Stir in broth and sesame seeds
7. When ready serve fried vegetables with the garlic mixture

ROASTED CAULIFLOWER

Serves: **2**

Prep Time: **10** Minutes

Cook Time: **30** Minutes

Total Time: **40** Minutes

INGREDIENTS

- 1 cauliflower head

BBQ SAUCE

- ¼ cup tomato sauce
- 1 tsp garam masala
- 1 tablespoon peanut butter
- 1 tsp olive oil
- 1 tsp Worchester sauce
- 1 tsp soy sauce
- 1 clove garlic
- 1 black pepper

DIRECTIONS

1. In a bowl combine all ingredients for the sauce and whisk well
2. Place the cauliflower in a baking dish and bake for 20-25 minutes at 225 F or until brown
3. When ready remove from the oven and serve with bbq sauce

GARLIC TOFU

Serves: **4**

Prep Time: **10**   Minutes

Cook Time: **20**   Minutes

Total Time: **30**   Minutes

INGREDIENTS

- 1 cup tofu
- 1 cup cooked brown rice
- 1 tablespoon chives
- 1 tablespoon olive oil
- 1 tsp vegan butter
- ¼ cup hoisin sauce
- 1 tablespoon soy sauce
- 2 cloves garlic
- 1 tsp sesame seeds

DIRECTIONS

1. In a bowl combine hoisin sauce, garlic and mix well
2. Add tofu, toss well and refrigerate overnight
3. In a skillet heat olive oil and add tofu and spread on a single layer
4. Add remaining ingredients, sprinkle sesame seeds and cook until browned

5. When ready remove from the pan and serve with brown rice

BUDDHA BOWL

Serves: **4**

Prep Time: **10** Minutes

Cook Time: **30** Minutes

Total Time: **40** Minutes

INGREDIENTS

- 1 cup buckwheat

DRESSING

- 1 tablespoon nutritional yeast
- 1 tsp mustard
- salt
- 1 clove garlic

DIRECTIONS

1. Place the buckwheat into a bowl and add 1-2 cups of water
2. In a blender all the ingredients for the dressing and blend until smooth
3. Divide the buckwheat between 2-3 plates and serve with dressing
4. Add toppings like tomatoes, bell pepper or radish sprouts

VEGAN RICE BACON

Serves: **4**

Prep Time: **10**   Minutes

Cook Time: **30**   Minutes

Total Time: **40**   Minutes

INGREDIENTS

- 2 rice paper sheets
- 1 tablespoon water
- 1 tablespoon olive oil
- 1 tablespoon soy sauce
- ¼ tsp onion powder
- ¼ tsp cumin powder
- 1 tsp tomato sauce
- 1 tsp agave syrup

DIRECTIONS

1. In a bowl combine all ingredients together excepting the rice paper
2. Dip the rice paper into a large plate with water
3. Cut the paper into strips and lay the strips onto a baking tray
4. Brush with sauce from the blender and bake for 10-12 minutes at 300 F
5. When ready remove from the oven and serve

FALAFEL BITES

Serves: **12**

Prep Time: **5** Minutes

Cook Time: **15** Minutes

Total Time: **20** Minutes

INGREDIENTS

- 1 cup chickpeas
- 1 onion
- ¼ cup parsley
- 2 cloves garlic
- 1 tsp baking soda
- 1 tablespoon flour
- 1 tsp cumin
- ¼ tsp coriander

DIRECTIONS

1. In a blender add all the ingredients and blend until smooth
2. In a pan heat olive oil and form small patties
3. Cook each falafel until crispy
4. When ready remove and serve

ZUCCHINI FRIES

Serves: *6*

Prep Time: *10*   Minutes

Cook Time: *20*   Minutes

Total Time: *30*   Minutes

INGREDIENTS

- 2 zucchinis
- ¼ cup breadcrumbs
- ¼ cup vegan cheese
- olive oil
- tahini
- pesto
- ketchup

DIRECTIONS

1. Cut zucchinis into thin strips
2. In a bowl add vegan cheese, breadcrumbs, salt and mix well
3. Dip each zucchini strip into the mixture
4. Place the strips onto a parchment paper
5. Bake for 18-20 minutes at 350 F
6. When ready remove from the oven and serve

ZUCCHINI DAL

Serves: 2

Prep Time: 5 Minutes

Cook Time: 20 Minutes

Total Time: 25 Minutes

INGREDIENTS

- 2 cups water
- ½ cup red lentils
- 1 zucchini
- 1 onion
- 2 tablespoons curry powder
- 1 tablespoon olive oil
- salt

DIRECTIONS

1. In a pot add zucchini, onion, pepper and sauté for 5-6 minutes
2. Ad lentils, water and the remaining ingredients
3. Cook on low heat for 15-18 minutes
4. When ready from heat, add scallions and serve

CHICKPEA PATTIES

Serves: **12**

Prep Time: **5** Minutes

Cook Time: **15** Minutes

Total Time: **20** Minutes

INGREDIENTS

- 2 lb. chickpeas
- ¼ cup parsley
- ½ red onion
- 2 tablespoons yeast flakes
- 2 tablespoons rosemary leaves
- olive oil

DIRECTIONS

1. Place chickpea in a blender and blend until smooth
2. Add remaining ingredients and blend again
3. Remove the mixture from the blender and form small patties

ONION SOUP

Serves: **4**

Prep Time: **10** Minutes

Cook Time: **20** Minutes

Total Time: **30** Minutes

INGREDIENTS

- 6 spring onions
- ½ red onion
- 1 potato
- 1 tablespoon olive oil
- Salt
- ¼ tsp coriander

DIRECTIONS

1. In a pot place the potatoes, water and boil until the potatoes are soft
2. In another pot heat olive oil and sauté spring onions and onion until soft
3. Add boiled potatoes to the pot where are the sauté onions
4. Add coriander, salt, pepper and stir well
5. Blend the soup until the soup is creamy
6. When ready pour into bowls and serve

ZUCCHINI SOUP

Serves: *6*

Prep Time: *10*   Minutes

Cook Time: 25   Minutes

Total Time: *35*   Minutes

INGREDIENTS

- 1 onion
- 1 tsp olive oil
- 1 zucchini
- 1 cup corn
- 1 cup broth
- 1 cup soy yogurt
- 1 tsp red pepper flakes
- 1 tablespoon cilantro
- 1 tablespoon parmesan

DIRECTIONS

1. In a skillet sauté onion until soft
2. Add zucchinis, corn and sauté for 5-6 minutes
3. Stir in water, vegetable broth, black pepper and salt
4. Bring everything to a boil and cook for 8-10 minutes
5. Add soy yogurt, cilantro, red pepper flakes and cook for another 5-6 minutes

SAUERKRAUT SOUP

Serves: **4**

Prep Time: **10**   Minutes

Cook Time: **30**   Minutes

Total Time: **40**   Minutes

INGREDIENTS

- 2 celery sticks
- 1 onion
- 2 carrots
- 2 potatoes
- 1 cup mushrooms
- 1 cup sauerkraut
- 6 cups vegetable broth
- 1 tablespoon olive oil
- 1 cup tofu
- 1 bay leaf

DIRECTIONS

1. In a pot heat olive oil and add tofu
2. Cook until crispy and set aside
3. Sauté onion and mushrooms for 2-3 minutes
4. Add vegetable broth and the rest of the ingredients

5. Bring everything to a boil and simmer on low heat for 18-20 minutes

6. When the soup is ready remove the bay leaf and transfer soup to a blender

7. Blend until smooth and serve with tofu slices on top

Serves: **6**

Prep Time: **10** Minutes

Cook Time: **35** Minutes

Total Time: **45** Minutes

INGREDIENTS

- 1 onion
- 1 carrot
- 1 cup celery
- 4 cups vegetable broth
- ¼ cup rice
- ½ cup tofu
- 1 tablespoon dill
- 1 lemon

EGG MIXTURE

- 1 cup coconut milk
- 1 cup tofu
- 2 tablespoons lemon juice
- 1 tsp salt
- 1 tsp black pepper
- 1 tsp nutritional yeast

DIRECTIONS

1. In a pot heat olive oil and add carrots, celery, onion and sauté until vegetables are soft

2. Add rice, vegetable broth and cook until the rice absorbs the liquid

3. In a blender add the ingredients for the egg mixture and blend until smooth

4. Pour the egg mixture into the soup and stir well

5. Add tofu, dill and any remaining ingredients to the soup

6. Cover and cook until the soup is ready

SALMON PIZZA

Serves: **6-8**

Prep Time: **10**   Minutes

Cook Time: **15**   Minutes

Total Time: **25**   Minutes

INGREDIENTS

- 1 pizza crust
- 1 shallot
- 1 parmesan cheese
- ½ red onion
- 2 tablespoons olive oil
- ½ lb. smoked salmon
- ½ lemon

DIRECTIONS

1. Spread tomato sauce on the pizza crust
2. Place all the toppings on the pizza crust
3. Bake the pizza at 425 F for 12-15 minutes
4. When ready remove pizza from the oven and serve

GREEN OLIVE PIZZA

Serves: **6-8**

Prep Time: **10** Minutes

Cook Time: **15** Minutes

Total Time: **25** Minutes

INGREDIENTS

- 1 onion
- 1 pizza crust
- 1 cup green olives
- 1 clove garlic
- ½ lb. potatoes
- ½ lb. taleggio

DIRECTIONS

1. Spread tomato sauce on the pizza crust
2. Place all the toppings on the pizza crust
3. Bake the pizza at 425 F for 12-15 minutes
4. When ready remove pizza from the oven and serve

CAULIFLOWER PIZZA

Serves: **6-8**

Prep Time: **10** Minutes

Cook Time: **15** Minutes

Total Time: **25** Minutes

INGREDIENTS

- 1 pizza crust
- 2 oz. parmesan cheese
- 1 tablespoon olive oil
- 4-5 basil leaves
- 1 cup mozzarella cheese
- 1 cup cauliflower

DIRECTIONS

1. Spread tomato sauce on the pizza crust
2. Place all the toppings on the pizza crust
3. Bake the pizza at 425 F for 12-15 minutes
4. When ready remove pizza from the oven and serve

ARTICHOKE AND SPINACH PIZZA

Serves: **6-8**

Prep Time: **10**   Minutes

Cook Time: **15**   Minutes

Total Time: **25**   Minutes

INGREDIENTS

- 1 pizza crust
- 1 garlic clove
- ½ lb. spinach
- ½ lb. soft cheese
- 2 oz. artichoke hearts
- 1 cup mozzarella cheese
- 1 tablespoon olive oil

DIRECTIONS

1. Spread tomato sauce on the pizza crust
2. Place all the toppings on the pizza crust
3. Bake the pizza at 425 F for 12-15 minutes
4. When ready remove pizza from the oven and serve

BEANS FRITATTA

Serves: **2**

Prep Time: **10** Minutes

Cook Time: **20** Minutes

Total Time: **30** Minutes

INGREDIENTS

- ½ lb. black beans
- 1 tablespoon olive oil
- ½ red onion
- ¼ tsp salt
- 2 eggs
- 2 oz. cheddar cheese
- 1 garlic clove
- ¼ tsp dill

DIRECTIONS

1. In a bowl whisk eggs with salt and cheese
2. In a frying pan heat olive oil and pour egg mixture
3. Add remaining ingredients and mix well
4. Serve when ready

SPINACH FRITATTA

Serves: **2**

Prep Time: **10** Minutes

Cook Time: **20** Minutes

Total Time: **30** Minutes

INGREDIENTS

- ½ lb. spinach
- 1 tablespoon olive oil
- ½ red onion
- ¼ tsp salt
- 2 eggs
- 2 oz. cheddar cheese
- 1 garlic clove
- ¼ tsp dill

DIRECTIONS

1. In a bowl whisk eggs with salt and cheese
2. In a frying pan heat olive oil and pour egg mixture
3. Add remaining ingredients and mix well
4. Serve when ready

ASIAN GREENS FRITATTA

Serves: **2**

Prep Time: **10** Minutes

Cook Time: **20** Minutes

Total Time: **30** Minutes

INGREDIENTS

- 1 cup Asian greens
- 1 tablespoon olive oil
- ½ red onion
- ¼ tsp salt
- 2 eggs
- 2 oz. cheddar cheese
- 1 garlic clove
- ¼ tsp dill

DIRECTIONS

1. In a bowl whisk eggs with salt and cheese
2. In a frying pan heat olive oil and pour egg mixture
3. Add remaining ingredients and mix well
4. Serve when ready

SALAMI FRITATTA

Serves: **2**

Prep Time: **10** Minutes

Cook Time: **20** Minutes

Total Time: **30** Minutes

INGREDIENTS

- 8-10 slices salami
- 1 tablespoon olive oil
- ½ red onion
- ¼ tsp salt
- 2 eggs
- 2 oz. parmesan cheese
- 1 garlic clove
- ¼ tsp dill

DIRECTIONS

1. In a bowl whisk eggs with salt and parmesan cheese
2. In a frying pan heat olive oil and pour egg mixture
3. Add remaining ingredients and mix well
4. When salami and eggs are cooked remove from heat and serve

BROCCOLI FRITATTA

Serves: **2**

Prep Time: **10** Minutes

Cook Time: **20** Minutes

Total Time: **30** Minutes

INGREDIENTS

- 1 cup broccoli
- 2 eggs
- 1 tablespoon olive oil
- ½ red onion
- ¼ tsp salt
- 2 oz. cheddar cheese
- 1 garlic clove
- ¼ tsp dill

DIRECTIONS

1. In a bowl whisk eggs with salt and cheese
2. In a frying pan heat olive oil and pour egg mixture
3. Add remaining ingredients and mix well
4. Serve when ready

VEGETARIAN CARBONARA

Serves: **2**

Prep Time: **10**   Minutes

Cook Time: **20**   Minutes

Total Time: **30**   Minutes

INGREDIENTS

- ¼ cup olive oil
- 1 tablespoon Worcestershire sauce
- 1 garlic clove
- 15 oz. spaghetti
- 1 cup water
- 2 eggs
- 1 tsp salt
- ½ cup parmesan cheese

DIRECTIONS

1. In a pot boil spaghetti until al dente
2. In another bowl whisk eggs with salt
3. Whisk ¼ cup pasta with egg mixture, garlic and pour a Dutch oven
4. When ready remove to a plate, add parmesan cheese and serve

KALE & QUINOA BOWL

Serves: 2

Prep Time: *10*   Minutes

Cook Time: *20*   Minutes

Total Time: *30*   Minutes

INGREDIENTS

- 1 cup cooked quinoa
- 1 bunch kale
- 2 tablespoons olive oil
- 1 cup tomatoes
- Juice from ½ lemon
- ¼ cup parmesan cheese

DIRECTIONS

1. Set cooked quinoa aside
2. In a pan heat olive oil and add kale
3. Add water and cook until tender
4. Place the cooked kale in a bowl
5. Add quinoa, tomatoes and lemon juice
6. Top with parmesan cheese and serve

AVOCADO TOAST

Serves: **1**

Prep Time: **5**   Minutes

Cook Time: **5**   Minutes

Total Time: **10**   Minutes

INGREDIENTS

- 2 slices gluten free toast
- 1 avocado
- 1 cup smoked salmon
- 6-8 basil leaves
- ¼ tsp salt

DIRECTIONS

1. Top bread with avocado and salmon
2. Add basil leaves, salt and top with another bread slice
3. Serve when ready

FIG & BRIE GRILLED CHEESE

Serves: 2

Prep Time: *10*   Minutes

Cook Time: *10*   Minutes

Total Time: *20*   Minutes

INGREDIENTS

- 1 tablespoon butter
- 4 slices bread
- 6 oz. brie cheese
- 2 figs

DIRECTIONS

1. In a pan heat olive oil
2. Divide the figs and cheese between 2 bread slices
3. Top with the other bread slices
4. Place in the pan and cover with a lid
5. Cook for 3-4 minutes per side on low heat
6. When ready remove from heat and serve

ROASTED SQUASH

Serves: **3-4**

Prep Time: **10**   Minutes

Cook Time: **20**   Minutes

Total Time: **30**   Minutes

INGREDIENTS

- 2 delicata squashes
- 2 tablespoons olive oil
- 1 tsp curry powder
- 1 tsp salt

DIRECTIONS

1. Preheat the oven to 400 F
2. Cut everything in half lengthwise
3. Toss everything with olive oil and place onto a prepared baking sheet
4. Roast for 18-20 minutes at 400 F or until golden brown
5. When ready remove from the oven and serve

Serves: *2*
Prep Time: *10*   Minutes

Cook Time: *20*   Minutes

Total Time: *30*   Minutes

INGREDIENTS

- 1 lb. brussels sprouts
- 1 tablespoon olive oil
- 1 tablespoon parmesan cheese
- 1 tsp garlic powder
- 1 tsp seasoning

DIRECTIONS

1. Preheat the oven to 425 F
2. In a bowl toss everything with olive oil and seasoning
3. Spread everything onto a prepared baking sheet
4. Bake for 8-10 minutes or until crisp
5. When ready remove from the oven and serve

PASTA

SIMPLE SPAGHETTI

Serves: 2

Prep Time: 5   Minutes

Cook Time: 15   Minutes

Total Time: 20   Minutes

INGREDIENTS

- 10 oz. spaghetti
- 2 eggs
- ½ cup parmesan cheese
- 1 tsp black pepper
- Olive oil
- 1 tsp parsley
- 2 cloves garlic

DIRECTIONS

1. In a pot boil spaghetti (or any other type of pasta), drain and set aside
2. In a bowl whish eggs with parmesan cheese
3. In a skillet heat olive oil, add garlic and cook for 1-2 minutes
4. Pour egg mixture and mix well
5. Add pasta and stir well

6. When ready garnish with parsley and serve

CHICKEN PASTA

Serves: *2*

Prep Time: *5*   Minutes

Cook Time: *15* Minutes

Total Time: *20* Minutes

INGREDIENTS

- 1 lb. cooked chicken breast
- 8 oz. pasta
- 2 tablespoons butter
- 1 tablespoon garlic
- 1 tablespoon flour
- ½ cup milk
- ½ cup heavy cream
- 1 jar red bell peppers
- 2 tablespoons basil

DIRECTIONS

1. In a pot boil spaghetti (or any other type of pasta), drain and set aside
2. Place all the ingredients for the sauce in a pot and bring to a simmer
3. Add pasta and mix well
4. When ready garnish with parmesan cheese and serve

Serves: 2

Prep Time: 5   Minutes

Cook Time: 15   Minutes

Total Time: 20   Minutes

INGREDIENTS

- ¼ cup mayonnaise
- ¼ cup sweet chili sauce
- 1 tablespoon lime juice
- 1 garlic clove
- 8 z. pasta
- 1 lb. shrimp
- ¼ tsp paprika

DIRECTIONS

1. In a pot boil spaghetti (or any other type of pasta), drain and set aside
2. Place all the ingredients for the sauce in a pot and bring to a simmer
3. Add pasta and mix well
4. When ready garnish with parmesan cheese and serve

PASTA WITH OLIVES AND TOMATOES

Serves: **2**

Prep Time: **5**   Minutes

Cook Time: **15** Minutes

Total Time: **20** Minutes

INGREDIENTS

- 8 oz. pasta
- 3 tablespoons olive oil
- 2 cloves garlic
- 5-6 anchovy fillets
- 2 cups tomatoes
- 1 cup olives
- ½ cup basil leaves

DIRECTIONS

1. In a pot boil spaghetti (or any other type of pasta), drain and set aside
2. Place all the ingredients for the sauce in a pot and bring to a simmer
3. Add pasta and mix well
4. When ready garnish with parmesan cheese and serve

GREEN SALAD WITH THAI DRESSING

Serves: *2*
Prep Time: *5*   Minutes

Cook Time: *5*   Minutes

Total Time: *10*   Minutes

INGREDIENTS

- 2 cucumber
- 10 cups salad greens
- 2 cups sunflower sprouts
- 2 stalks celery

DRESSING

- ½ cup lime juice
- 2 tablespoons fish sauce
- ¼ tsp honey
- 1 clove garlic
- 1 tablespoon cilantro

DIRECTIONS

1. In a bowl combine all ingredients together and mix well
2. Serve with dressing

198

CRANBERRY KALE SALAD

Serves: **2**

Prep Time: **5** Minutes

Cook Time: **5** Minutes

Total Time: **10** Minutes

INGREDIENTS

- 6 oz. bacon
- 1 bunches of kale
- ¾ cup dried cranberries
- ½ cup olive oil
- ½ cup red onion

DIRECTIONS

1. In a bowl combine all ingredients together and mix well
2. Serve with salad dressing

AVOCADO AND SHRIMP SALAD

Serves: 2

Prep Time: 5   Minutes

Cook Time: 5   Minutes

Total Time: *10*   Minutes

INGREDIENTS

- 3 tablespoons lime juice
- 2 tablespoons olive oil
- ¼ cup cilantro
- ¼ tsp cracked pepper
- 1 pinch salt

DIRECTIONS

1. In a bowl combine all ingredients together and mix well
2. Serve with salad dressing

FENNEL SALAD

Serves: 2

Prep Time: 5   Minutes

Cook Time: 5   Minutes

Total Time: *10*   Minutes

INGREDIENTS

- 1 lb. fennel
- juice 1 lemon
- ½ tsp salt
- 1 tablespoon olive oil

DIRECTIONS

1. In a bowl combine all ingredients together and mix well
2. Serve with salad dressing

Serves: 2

Prep Time: 5   Minutes

Cook Time: 5   Minutes

Total Time: 10   Minutes

INGREDIENTS

- 2 cups kale
- 1 tablespoon coconut oil
- 2 cups spinach
- ½ cup dried cranberries
- 1 tablespoon sliced almonds
- 1 tablespoon water

DIRECTIONS

1. In a bowl combine all ingredients together and mix well
2. Serve with salad dressing

GREEN SALAD

Serves: 2

Prep Time: 5 Minutes

Cook Time: 5 Minutes

Total Time: *10* Minutes

INGREDIENTS

- 12 cup salad greens
- 1 bunch radishes
- ½ onion
- 1 cucumber

ITALIAN DRESSING

- 5 tablespoons olive oil
- ½ cup apple cider vinegar
- ½ tsp oregano leaves
- ½ tsp rosemary
- ½ tsp marjoram leaves
- ½ tsp thyme leaves
- 1 clove garlic

DIRECTIONS

1. In a bowl combine all ingredients together and mix well
2. Serve with salad dressing

CUCUMBER SALAD

Serves: **4**

Prep Time: **5** Minutes

Cook Time: **5** Minutes

Total Time: **10** Minutes

INGREDIENTS

- 1 cucumber
- 1 tsp salt
- 3 green onions
- 1 tablespoon cilantro
- ½ cup lemon juice
- ½ cup olive oil
- 1 tsp lemon zest
- ¼ tsp cracked pepper

DIRECTIONS

1. In a bowl mix all ingredients and mix well
2. Serve with salad dressing

APRICOT SALAD

Serves: **4**

Prep Time: **5**   Minutes

Cook Time: **5**   Minutes

Total Time: **10**   Minutes

INGREDIENTS

- 2 apricots
- 5 cups arugula

BALSAMIC VINAIGRETTE

- ½ cup balsamic vinegar
- ½ cup olive oil
- 3 tsp mustard
- 1 tablespoon chives

DIRECTIONS

1. In a bowl mix all ingredients and mix well
2. Serve with salad dressing

MORNING SALAD

Serves: 2

Prep Time: 5   Minutes

Cook Time: 5   Minutes

Total Time: *10*   Minutes

INGREDIENTS

- 1 onion
- 1 tsp cumin
- 1 tablespoon olive oil
- 1 avocado
- ¼ lb. cooked lentils
- 1 oz. walnuts
- Coriander
- ¼ lb. feta cheese
- Salad dressing of choice
- 8-10 baby carrots

DIRECTIONS

1. In a bowl combine all ingredients together and mix well
2. Add dressing and serve

FIFTH COOKBOOK

ZUCCHINI SOUP

Serves: *4*

Prep Time: *10*   Minutes

Cook Time: *20*   Minutes

Total Time: *30*   Minutes

INGREDIENTS

- 1 tablespoon olive oil
- 1 lb. zucchini
- ¼ red onion
- ½ cup all-purpose flour
- ¼ tsp salt
- ¼ tsp pepper
- 1 can vegetable broth
- 1 cup heavy cream

DIRECTIONS

1. In a saucepan heat olive oil and sauté zucchini until tender
2. Add remaining ingredients to the saucepan and bring to a boil

3. When all the vegetables are tender transfer to a blender and blend until smooth

4. Pour soup into bowls, garnish with parsley and serve

CUCUMBER SOUP

Serves: *2*

Prep Time: *10*   Minutes

Cook Time: *20*   Minutes

Total Time: *30*   Minutes

INGREDIENTS

- 2 tablespoons olive oil
- 2 cloves garlic
- ¼ cup lemon juice
- ¼ cup parsley
- ¼. cup cilantro
- ¼ cup greens
- 1 cup baby spinach
- 2 cups cucumber
- Salt
- radishes

DIRECTIONS

1. In a blender add all ingredients and blend until smooth
2. Season and refrigerate the soup
3. When ready pour soup into bowl and serve

VEGETARIAN MINESTRONE SOUP

Serves: **5**

Prep Time: **10**   Minutes

Cook Time: **40**   Minutes

Total Time: **50**   Minutes

INGREDIENTS

- 1 tablespoon olive oil
- ¾ cup onion
- 2 ½ cups water
- 2 cups zucchini
- 1 cup sliced carrots
- 1 cup beans
- ¼ cup celery
- 2 tablespoons basil
- 1/3 tsp oregano
- ¼ tsp black pepper
- 1 can plum tomatoes
- 2 cloves garlic
- ½ cup uncooked pasta

DIRECTIONS

1. In a saucepan add oil, onion and sauté for 4-5 minutes

2. Add remaining ingredients and bring to a boil
3. Reduce heat and simmer on low heat for 20-25 minutes
4. Add pasta and cook until pasta is al dente for 10-12 minutes
5. When ready, remove from heat and serve

CABBAGE STEW

Serves: **4**

Prep Time: **10**   Minutes

Cook Time: **40**   Minutes

Total Time: **50**   Minutes

INGREDIENTS

- 1 lb. bison
- 1 tablespoon olive oil
- ¼ cabbage
- 2 carrots
- 1 onion
- 2 cloves garlic
- 2 tablespoons aminos
- 4 cups chicken stock

DIRECTIONS

1. In a pot sauté the carrot, onion and cabbage for 2-3 minutes
2. Add bison and cook for 4-5 minutes
3. Add chicken stock, garlic, ginger and coconut aminos
4. Cook for 25-30 minutes
5. When ready from heat garnish with pepper and serve

CHICKEN RICE SOUP

Serves: **4**

Prep Time: **10** Minutes

Cook Time: **40** Minutes

Total Time: **50** Minutes

INGREDIENTS

- 1 tablespoon olive oil
- 1 cup carrot
- 1 cup onion
- 1 cup celery
- 1 chicken breast
- 2 cloves garlic
- 6 cups chicken broth
- ½ cup brown rice
- ¼ cup lemon juice
- 1 tsp black pepper
- ¼ cup parsley

DIRECTIONS

1. In a pot sauté the carrot, onion and celery for 2-3 minutes
2. Add chicken breast and cook for another 4-5 minutes
3. Add rice, lemon juice, pepper and chicken broth

4. Cook for 30-40 minutes on high heat
5. When soup is cooked remove from heat
6. Garnish with parsley and serve

MISO SOUP

Serves: *2*

Prep Time: *10*   Minutes

Cook Time: *20*   Minutes

Total Time: *30*   Minutes

INGREDIENTS

- 2 tablespoons arame
- 1 cup water
- 2 cups chicken broth
- 1 cup mushrooms
- 2 tablespoons miso paste
- 10 oz. codfish fillet
- 2 cups vegetables
- ¼ cup broccoli sprouts
- 1 tablespoon scallion
- 1 tablespoon olive oil

DIRECTIONS

1. In a bowl soak arame and set aside
2. In a saucepan add broth and bring to a boil
3. Add the cod to the saucepan, vegetables. cover and cook for 5-6 minutes
4. Stir in the miso paste and cook until soup is ready

5. Ladle into bowls top with scallions and serve

MUSHROOM SOUP

Serves: **6**

Prep Time: **20** Minutes

Cook Time: **35** Minutes

Total Time: **55** Minutes

INGREDIENTS

- 2 tablespoons olive oil
- 2 onions
- 2 celery sticks
- 4 garlic cloves
- 4 sprigs of rosemary
- 3 carrots
- 3 cups mushrooms
- 4 cups vegetable broth
- 2 bay leaves

DIRECTIONS

1. In a saucepan sauté garlic, celery, onions until soft
2. Add mushrooms, carrots and sauté for another 4-5 minutes
3. Add bay leaves, broth and simmer for 25-30 minutes
4. When ready remove from heat and serve

CHICKEN SOUP

Serves: **4**

Prep Time: **15**   Minutes

Cook Time: **50**   Minutes

Total Time: **65**   Minutes

INGREDIENTS

- 1 chicken
- 2 tablespoons coconut oil
- 2 l water
- 2 tablespoons apple cider vinegar
- 2 onions
- 6 carrots
- 5 celery sticks
- 2 zucchinis
- 1-inch ginger root
- 4 cloves garlic
- 1 bunch parsley

DIRECTIONS

1. Cut chicken into pieces and place in a pot
2. Add water, vinegar, parsley and boil for 50-60 minutes
3. Meanwhile add the rest of the ingredients

4. Simmer for 5-6 hours on low heat
5. When ready remove from heat and serve

ASPARAGUS SOUP

Serves: **4**

Prep Time: **10** Minutes

Cook Time: **50** Minutes

Total Time: **60** Minutes

INGREDIENTS

- 8 oz. fennel bulbs
- 10 oz. asparagus
- 1 bunch onions
- 3 cups water
- 1 tsp salt
- 2 tablespoons rice
- 2 leeks
- 2 tablespoons sesame oil
- ¼ cup dill
- ¼ cup mint leaves
- 2 cups vegetable broth
- 2 tablespoons lemon juice

DIRECTIONS

1. In a skillet heat olive oil and sauté onion, dill and mint leaves
2. Slice the vegetables and place them in a pot

3. Add salt, rice, water and simmer for 35-45 minutes

4. Add sautéed ingredients to the soup and simmer for another 4-5 minutes

5. When ready blend the soup and serve

SEASWEED SOUP

Serves: **2**
Prep Time: **15**   Minutes

Cook Time: **20**   Minutes

Total Time: **35**   Minutes

INGREDIENTS

- 2 cups water
- 1 tablespoon soy sauce
- 2 oz. seaweed
- ¼ cup tofu
- 1-inch ginger
- 1 tsp olive oil
- 2 garlic cloves
- 4 scallions

DIRECTIONS

1. In a soup pot add water, scallion, ginger, garlic and bring to a boil
2. In a skillet heat olive oil and sauté tofu
3. Add sautéed tofu to the soup and the rest of the ingredients
4. Cook until soup is cooked
5. When ready remove from heat garnish with scallions and serve

SESAME PORK TACOS

Serves: **4**

Prep Time: **5**   Minutes

Cook Time: **15**   Minutes

Total Time: **25**   Minutes

INGREDIENTS

- 1 cup cucumber slices
- 5 radishes
- ½ cup red wine vinegar
- 3 tsp sugar
- 1 tablespoon olive oil
- 3 scallions
- 1 cup red cabbage
- 1 lb. ground pork
- 2 tsp garlic powder
- 2 tablespoons sesame oil
- 2 tablespoons soy sauce
- 1 tsp Sriracha
- 10 tortillas
- 1 tsp cilantro
- ¼ cup sour cream

DIRECTIONS

1. In a bowl add radishes, cucumbers, vinegar, 1 tsp sugar and salt, stir well to combine
2. In a pan add oil, scallions, cabbage and cook for 4-5 minutes
3. Add pork, sugar, garlic powder and cook for another 4-5 minutes
4. Add soy sauce, sesame oil and stir to combine
5. Spread sour cream in the center of your tortilla, add pork filling and sprinkle cilantro, radishes and top with meat mixture

WATERMELON GAZPACHO

Serves: **3**

Prep Time: **10**   Minutes

Cook Time: **10**   Minutes

Total Time: **20**   Minutes

INGREDIENTS

- 2 cups ripe watermelon
- 1 red pepper
- ¼ onion
- 3 tablespoons red wine vinegar
- 6 tablespoons cranberry juice
- Italian basil leaves as needed

DIRECTIONS

1. Puree all ingredients, except the basil, until smooth
2. Refrigerate to chill
3. Serve garnished with basil, onion, tomato or cucumber

LIME GRILLED CORN

Serves: *3*
Prep Time: *5*   Minutes

Cook Time: *15*   Minutes

Total Time: *20*   Minutes

INGREDIENTS

- 3 ears of corn
- 2 tablespoons mayonnaise
- 2 tablespoons squeezed lime juice
- ½ tsp chili powder
- 1 pinch of salt

DIRECTIONS

1. Place corn onto the grill and cook for 5-6 minutes or until the kernels being to brown
2. Turn every few minutes until all sides are slightly charred
3. In a bowl mix the rest of ingredients
4. Spread a light coating of the mixture onto each cob and serve

MACADAMIA DIP WITH VEGETABLES

Serves: **4**

Prep Time: **10** Minutes

Cook Time: **30** Minutes

Total Time: **40** Minutes

INGREDIENTS

- 6 oz. squash
- ½ bunch basil
- ¼ cup macadamia nuts
- 1 tablespoon olive oil
- ¼ lemon
- ¼ tsp ground smoked paprika
- salt
- vegetable sticks

DIRECTIONS

1. Preheat the oven to 350 F
2. Cut the squash into chunks and roast for 25-30 minutes
3. In a food processor add the basil leaves, lemon zest, macadamia nuts, squash pieces and salt
4. Serve with vegetable sticks: cucumber, carrots, tomatoes and green pepper

GINGERSNAPS

Serves: **6**

Prep Time: **10**   Minutes

Cook Time: **15**   Minutes

Total Time: **25**   Minutes

INGREDIENTS

- 1 cup white whole wheat flour
- 1 cornstarch
- 1 tsp baking powder
- 1 tsp ground ginger
- ½ tsp ground cinnamon
- ¼ tsp nutmeg
- ¼ tsp ground cloves
- 1 tablespoon unsalted butter
- 1 egg white
- 2 tsp vanilla stevia
- ½ cup nonfat milk
- ½ cup molasses
- 1 tsp vanilla extract

DIRECTIONS

1. **Preheat the oven to 350 F**

2. In a bowl whisk together the cornstarch, ginger, baking powder, cinnamon, nutmeg, cloves and salt and flour

3. In another bowl mix vanilla extract, egg, butter, stevia, molasses and milk

4. Add in the flour mixture and stir until fully incorporated

5. Divide dough into 14-16 portions and roll each into a ball

6. Place onto a baking sheet and press it down into the cookie dough

7. Bake for 8-10 minutes

8. When ready, remove and serve

TURKEY & VEGGIES STUFFED PEPPERS

Serves: **4**

Prep Time: **10**   Minutes

Cook Time: **40**   Minutes

Total Time: **50**   Minutes

INGREDIENTS

- 4 red bell peppers
- 1 lb. ground turkey
- 1 tablespoon olive oil
- ¼ onion
- 1 cup mushrooms 1 zucchini
- ½ green bell pepper
- ½ yellow bell pepper
- 1 cup spinach
- 1 can diced tomatoes
- 1 tsp Italian seasoning
- ¼ tsp garlic powder
- 1 pinch of salt

DIRECTIONS

1. Preheat the oven to 325 F
2. In a pot bring water to boil, add pepper and cook for 5-6 minutes

3. In a skillet cook the turkey until brown and set aside
4. In another pan add onion, olive oil, mushrooms, zucchini, green, yellow pepper, spinach and cook until tender
5. Add remaining ingredients to the turkey and cook until done
6. Stuff the peppers with the mixture and place them into a casserole dish
7. Bake for 15-18 minutes or until done

QUINOA TACO MEAT

Serves: **6**

Prep Time: **10** Minutes

Cook Time: **50** Minutes

Total Time: **60** Minutes

INGREDIENTS

- 1 cup red quinoa
- 1 cup vegetable broth
- ¾ cup water

SEASONING

- ¼ cup salsa
- 1 tablespoon yeast
- 1 tsp cumin
- 1 tsp chili powder
- ¼ tsp garlic powder
- ½ tsp black pepper
- ½ tsp salt
- 1 tablespoon olive oil

DIRECTIONS

1. In a saucepan add quinoa and cook for 5-6 minutes
2. Add water, vegetable broth and bring to a boil

3. Reduce heat to low and cook for 20-22 minutes or until liquid is absorbed

4. Add quinoa to a mixing bowl, remaining ingredients and toss to combine

5. Bake for 25-30 minutes or until golden brown

6. When ready remove and serve with taco salads, enchiladas or nachos

KALE CHIPS

Serves: *6*

Prep Time: *10* Minutes

Cook Time: 25 Minutes

Total Time: 35 Minutes

INGREDIENTS

- 1 bunch of kale
- 1 tablespoon olive oil
- 1 tsp salt

DIRECTIONS

1. Preheat the oven to 325 F
2. Chop the kale into chip size pieces
3. Put pieces into a bowl tops with olive oil and salt
4. Spread the leaves in a single layer onto a parchment paper
5. Bake for 20-25 minutes
6. When ready, remove and serve

CHICKEN AND BROWN RICE PASTA

Serves: 2

Prep Time: **10** Minutes

Cook Time: **15** Minutes

Total Time: **25** Minutes

INGREDIENTS

- 1 cup cooked rice pasta
- 1 chicken breast
- ¼ cup no sugar marinara sauce
- ½ cup tomatoes
- parsley for serving
- 1 tsp olive oil

DIRECTIONS

1. In a skillet cook the pasta according to the package directions
2. Drain and rinse the pasta
3. Add cooked chicken breast, marinara sauce and serve

PHILLY CHEESE STEAK

Serves: **4**

Prep Time: **5**   Minutes

Cook Time: **20**   Minutes

Total Time: **25**   Minutes

INGREDIENTS

- 2 tsp olive oil
- 1 onion
- 3 portobello mushrooms
- 1 red bell pepper
- 1 tsp dried oregano
- ¼ tsp ground pepper
- 1 tablespoon all-purpose flour
- ½ cup vegetable broth
- 1 tablespoon soy sauce
- 2 oz. vegan cheese
- 3 whole-wheat rolls

DIRECTIONS

1. In a skillet add onion, pepper, bell pepper, oregano and cook until soft
2. Reduce heat, sprinkle flour, soy sauce, broth and bring to a simmer

3. Remove from heat, add cheese slices on top and let it stand until fully melted

4. Divide into 3-4 portions and serve

CAULIFLOWER WINGS

Serves: **4**

Prep Time: **10** Minutes

Cook Time: **50** Minutes

Total Time: **60** Minutes

INGREDIENTS

- 1 head cauliflower
- ¼ unsweetened almond milk
- ¼ cup water
- ¾ rice flour
- 1 tsp garlic powder
- 1 tsp onion powder
- 1 tsp cumin
- 1 tsp paprika
- ½ tsp salt
- ¼ tsp ground pepper
- bbq sauce

VINEGAR SAUCE

- 1 tablespoon vegan butter
- 2 tablespoons apple cider vinegar
- 1 tablespoon water
- 1 pinch of salt

DIRECTIONS

1. Preheat the oven to 425 F
2. Mix all wing ingredients in a bowl and submerge each cauliflower floret into the mix
3. Place florets on a prepare baking sheet
4. Bake for 10 minutes, flip and bake for another 10 minutes or until golden brown
5. Remove the cauliflower from the oven and serve with vinegar sauce
6. When ready season with pepper and salt and serve

ROASTED BOK CHOY

Serves: **4**

Prep Time: **5**   Minutes

Cook Time: **15**   Minutes

Total Time: **20**   Minutes

INGREDIENTS

- 5 heads baby bok choy
- olive oil
- 1 tsp pepper
- 1 tsp salt

DIRECTIONS

1. Preheat the oven to 425 F
2. Cut each bok choy in half lengthwise and place on a baking sheet
3. Drizzle with olive oil, pepper and salt
4. Bake for 10-12 minutes, flip and bake for another 8-10 minutes
5. When ready remove and serve

Serves: 2

Prep Time: 5   Minutes

Cook Time: 15   Minutes

Total Time: 20   Minutes

INGREDIENTS

- 4 oz. spaghetti
- 2 cups basil leaves
- 2 garlic cloves
- ¼ cup olive oil
- 2 tablespoons parmesan cheese
- ½ tsp black pepper

DIRECTIONS

1. Bring water to a boil and add pasta
2. In a blend add parmesan cheese, basil leaves, garlic and blend
3. Add olive oil, pepper and blend again
4. Pour pesto onto pasta and serve when ready

TACO SALAD

Serves: *2*

Prep Time: *5*   Minutes

Cook Time: *5*   Minutes

Total Time: *10*   Minutes

INGREDIENTS

- ½ cup olive oil
- 1 lb. cooked steak
- 1 tablespoon taco seasoning
- Juice of 1 lime
- 1 tsp cumin
- 1 head romaine lettuce
- 1 cup corn
- 1 cup beans
- 1 cup tomatoes

DIRECTIONS

1. In a bowl mix all ingredients and mix well
2. Serve with dressing

KALE SALAD

Serves: 2

Prep Time: 5 Minutes

Cook Time: 5 Minutes

Total Time: *10* Minutes

INGREDIENTS

- 2 cups kale
- 1 tablespoon hemp seeds
- 1 cucumber
- 1 tsp honey
- 1 tsp olive oil
- 1 handful parsley

DIRECTIONS

1. In a bowl mix all ingredients and mix well
2. Serve with dressing

Serves: 2

Prep Time: 5   Minutes

Cook Time: 5   Minutes

Total Time: *10*   Minutes

INGREDIENTS

- 1 cup cauliflower
- 1 cup broccoli
- 1 cup brussels sprouts
- 1 cup red bell pepper
- 1 cup squash
- 1 tablespoon olive oil

DIRECTIONS

1. In a bowl mix all ingredients and mix well
2. Serve with dressing

Serves: *2*

Prep Time: *5* Minutes

Cook Time: *5* Minutes

Total Time: *10* Minutes

INGREDIENTS

- ½ cauliflower florets
- 1 cup pumpkin
- 1 cup Brussel sprouts
- 1 cup quinoa
- 1 tablespoon olive oil

DIRECTIONS

1. In a bowl mix all ingredients and mix well
2. Serve with dressing

Serves: 2

Prep Time: 5   Minutes

Cook Time: 5   Minutes

Total Time: 10   Minutes

INGREDIENTS

- 2 red chicory
- 2 fennel bulbs
- ½ cup watercress
- 2 garlic cloves
- 1 tablespoon olive oil

DIRECTIONS

1. In a bowl mix all ingredients and mix well
2. Serve with dressing

FENNEL SALAD

Serves: 2

Prep Time: 5   Minutes

Cook Time: 5   Minutes

Total Time: 10 Minutes

INGREDIENTS

- 1 fennel bulb
- 1 tablespoon lemon juice
- ¼ cup olive oil
- 1 tsp mint
- 1 tsp onion

DIRECTIONS

1. In a bowl mix all ingredients and mix well
2. Serve with dressing

GIGNER CILANTRO SALAD

Serves: 2

Prep Time: 5   Minutes

Cook Time: 5   Minutes

Total Time: 10 Minutes

INGREDIENTS

- 2 lb. sweet potatoes
- ¼ cup olive oil
- 2 tablespoons lemon juice
- ¼ cup scallions
- ¼ cup cilantro
- ¼ tsp salt

DIRECTIONS

1. In a bowl mix all ingredients and mix well
2. Serve with dressing

WATERCRESS FRITATTA

Serves: 2

Prep Time: **10** Minutes

Cook Time: **20** Minutes

Total Time: **30** Minutes

INGREDIENTS

- ½ lb. watercress
- 1 tablespoon olive oil
- ½ red onion
- ¼ tsp salt
- 2 oz. cheddar cheese
- 1 garlic clove
- ¼ tsp dill

DIRECTIONS

1. In a bowl whisk eggs with salt and cheese
2. In a frying pan heat olive oil and pour egg mixture
3. Add remaining ingredients and mix well
4. Serve when ready

KALE FRITATTA

Serves: *2*

Prep Time: *10* Minutes

Cook Time: *20* Minutes

Total Time: *30* Minutes

INGREDIENTS

- 1 cup kale
- 1 tablespoon olive oil
- ½ red onion
- ¼ tsp salt
- 2 oz. cheddar cheese
- 1 garlic clove
- ¼ tsp dill

DIRECTIONS

1. In a skillet sauté kale until tender
2. In a bowl whisk eggs with salt and cheese
3. In a frying pan heat olive oil and pour egg mixture
4. Add remaining ingredients and mix well
5. When ready serve with sautéed kale

MEDITERRANENA BUDDA BOWL

Serves: **1**

Prep Time: **10** Minutes

Cook Time: **10** Minutes

Total Time: **20** Minutes

INGREDIENTS

- 1 zucchini
- ¼ tsp oregano
- Salt
- 1 cup cooked quinoa
- 1 cup spinach
- 1 cup mixed greens
- ½ cup red pepper
- ¼ cup cucumber
- ¼ cup tomatoes
- parsley
- tahini dressing

DIRECTIONS

1. In a skillet heat olive oil olive and sauté zucchini until soft and sprinkle oregano over zucchini

2. In a bowl add the rest of ingredients and toss to combine
3. Add fried zucchini and mix well
4. Pour over tahini dressing, mix well and serve

VEGAN CURRY

Serves: *4*

Prep Time: *10* Minutes

Cook Time: *20* Minutes

Total Time: *30* Minutes

INGREDIENTS

- 1 tablespoon olive oil
- ¼ cup onion
- 2 stalks celery
- 1 garlic clove
- ¼ tsp coriander
- ¼ tsp cumin
- ¼ tsp turmeric
- ¼ tsp red pepper flakes
- 1 cauliflower
- 1 zucchini
- 2 tomatoes
- 1 tsp salt
- 1 cup vegetable broth
- 1 handful of baby spinach
- 1 tablespoon almonds
- 1 tablespoon cilantro

DIRECTIONS

1. In a skillet heat olive oil and sauté celery, garlic and onions for 4-5 minutes or until vegetables are tender

2. Add cumin, spices, coriander, cumin, turmeric red pepper flakes stir to combine and cook for another 1-2 minutes

3. Add zucchini, cauliflower, tomatoes, broth, spinach, water and simmer on low heat for 15-20 minutes

4. Add remaining ingredients and simmer for another 4-5 minutes

5. Garnish curry and serve

Serves: 2

Prep Time: 5   Minutes

Cook Time: 15   Minutes

Total Time: 20   Minutes

INGREDIENTS

- 1 cauliflower
- 1 tablespoon rosemary
- 1 cup vegetable stock
- 2 garlic cloves
- salt

DIRECTIONS

1. In a saucepan add cauliflower, stock and bring to a boil for 12-15 minutes
2. Blend cauliflower until smooth, add garlic, salt, rosemary and blend again
3. When ready pour in a bowl and serve

BRUSSELS SPROUTS

Serves: *2*

Prep Time: *10* Minutes

Cook Time: *20* Minutes

Total Time: *30* Minutes

INGREDIENTS

- 1 tablespoon olive oil
- 2 shallots
- 2 cloves garlic
- 1 lb. brussels sprouts
- 1 cup vegetable stock
- 4 springs thyme
- ¼ cup pine nuts

DIRECTIONS

1. In a pan heat olive oil and cook shallots until tender
2. Add garlic, sprouts, thyme, stock and cook for another 4-5 minutes
3. Cover and cook for another 10-12 minutes or until sprouts are soft
4. When ready add pine nuts and serve

PIZZA

SIMPLE PIZZA RECIPE

Serves: **6-8**

Prep Time: **10**   Minutes

Cook Time: **15**   Minutes

Total Time: **25**   Minutes

INGREDIENTS

- 1 pizza crust
- ½ cup tomato sauce
- ¼ black pepper
- 1 cup pepperoni slices
- 1 cup mozzarella cheese
- 1 cup olives

DIRECTIONS

1. Spread tomato sauce on the pizza crust
2. Place all the toppings on the pizza crust
3. Bake the pizza at 425 F for 12-15 minutes
4. When ready remove pizza from the oven and serve

ZUCCHINI PIZZA

Serves: **6-8**

Prep Time: **10**   Minutes

Cook Time: **15**   Minutes

Total Time: **25**   Minutes

INGREDIENTS

- 1 pizza crust
- ½ cup tomato sauce
- ¼ black pepper
- 1 cup zucchini slices
- 1 cup mozzarella cheese
- 1 cup olives

DIRECTIONS

1. Spread tomato sauce on the pizza crust
2. Place all the toppings on the pizza crust
3. Bake the pizza at 425 F for 12-15 minutes
4. When ready remove pizza from the oven and serve

CAULIFLOWER RECIPE

Serves: *6-8*

Prep Time: *10*   Minutes

Cook Time: *15*   Minutes

Total Time: *25*   Minutes

INGREDIENTS

- 1 pizza crust
- ½ cup tomato sauce
- ¼ black pepper
- 1 cup cauliflower
- 1 cup mozzarella cheese
- 1 cup olives

DIRECTIONS

1. Spread tomato sauce on the pizza crust
2. Place all the toppings on the pizza crust
3. Bake the pizza at 425 F for 12-15 minutes
4. When ready remove pizza from the oven and serve

Serves: *6-8*
Prep Time: *10*   Minutes

Cook Time: *15*   Minutes

Total Time: *25*   Minutes

INGREDIENTS

- 1 pizza crust
- ½ cup tomato sauce
- ¼ black pepper
- 1 cup broccoli
- 1 cup mozzarella cheese
- 1 cup olives

DIRECTIONS

1. Spread tomato sauce on the pizza crust
2. Place all the toppings on the pizza crust
3. Bake the pizza at 425 F for 12-15 minutes
4. When ready remove pizza from the oven and serve

TOMATOES & HAM PIZZA

Serves: **6-8**

Prep Time: **10** Minutes

Cook Time: **15** Minutes

Total Time: **25** Minutes

INGREDIENTS

- 1 pizza crust
- ½ cup tomato sauce
- ¼ black pepper
- 1 cup pepperoni slices
- 1 cup tomatoes
- 6-8 ham slices
- 1 cup mozzarella cheese
- 1 cup olives

DIRECTIONS

1. Spread tomato sauce on the pizza crust
2. Place all the toppings on the pizza crust
3. Bake the pizza at 425 F for 12-15 minutes
4. When ready remove pizza from the oven and serve

THANK YOU FOR READING THIS BOOK!

CPSIA information can be obtained
at www.ICGtesting.com
Printed in the USA
BVHW072049140521
607266BV00002B/206